LOST
CIVILIZATIONS

LOST
CIVILIZATIONS

BILL HARRIS

Friedman Group

A FRIEDMAN GROUP BOOK

Copyright © 1993 by Michael Friedman Publishing Group, Inc.

ISBN 0-7924-5842-7

LOST CIVILIZATIONS
was prepared and produced by
Michael Friedman Publishing Group, Inc.
15 West 26th Street
New York, New York 10010

Editor: Nathaniel Marunas
Art Director: Jeff Batzli
Designer: Patrick McCarthy
Layout: Philip Travisano
Photography Editor: Anne K. Price

Typeset by Bookworks Plus
Color separations by Rainbow Graphic Arts Co., Ltd.
Printed in Hong Kong and bound in China by Leefung-Asco Printers Ltd.

ACKNOWLEDGMENTS

With heartfelt thanks to Nathaniel Marunas
and the entire staff at the Michael Friedman Publishing Group
for their guidance and for their civilized patience.
And to the people at the Greenwich, Connecticut, Public Library
for their amazing collection of materials
on civilizations lost and found.

Contents

Introduction
The Beginning of Time

About three hundred years ago, an Irish bishop claimed to have solved the riddle of the ages when he announced that the first human, Adam, was created on October 22, 4004 B.C. at eight o'clock in the evening. He arrived at this conclusion by analyzing the life spans of people mentioned in the Bible. Given the nature of his inquiry, however, his figures could have been wrong and it wasn't too surprising when his findings were challenged by an English mathematician. According to the revised version, the human experience began a day later at nine o'clock in the morning. Either way, it became an accepted fact in the seventeenth century that the history of humankind didn't extend back in time much more than 5,600 years. In the years since, paleoanthropologists have produced evidence that the ancestors of the species we call *Homo sapiens* were walking upright as far back as two million years ago and they are certain that modern man appeared on earth between 350,000 and 500,000 years ago. But archaeologists still haven't found evidence of cultures with written histories dating back more than 6,000 years. For now at least, there is no proof that humans capable of creating a civilization as we define it existed before then.

ATLANTIS

There is, however, another country, another continent, to be considered. If the stories are true, there was a highly civilized race living in the island kingdom of Atlantis some 12,000 years ago. This is an idea that has been alternately believed and discredited over the centuries. There exists in the oral tradition of the Vikings references to a mystical island called Atli and a similar reference in ancient Indian writings to the White Island, Attala. When the Spanish arrived in the Americas, they found a tribe that claimed its ancestors were from a place they called Atlàn. Phoenicians, who had traded with the ancestors of the Spanish, believed the Iberians to be the remnants of a lost tribe that once lived on a huge island they called Antila. Among some ancient Arabic cultures, the island was known as Ad, which could have been the root of the name Adam, whom the Book of Genesis tells us is our oldest ancestor.

Believers in the legend of Atlantis base their belief on the dialogues of the Greek philosopher Plato. Writing in about 360 B.C., he re-created a conversation that took place thirty years earlier between his

BUILT ON TOP OF CAPE SOUNION NEAR THE SOUTHERN EDGE OF THE CITY OF ATHENS, THIS TEMPLE (OPPOSITE PAGE) HONORING THE SEA GOD POSEIDON WAS THE FIRST SIGHT THAT GREETED SHIPS BRINGING CARGO AND PASSENGERS THROUGH THE PORT OF PIRAEUS IN THE FOURTH CENTURY B.C.

SUNKEN TREASURE

If the lost continent of Atlantis is found under the sea, any artifacts made of gold will probably be intact because gold doesn't corrode. As divers exploring shipwrecks have discovered, however, silver does not last forever in the briny deep, and any Atlantean silver will probably long since have been transformed into compounds of chloride or bromide. The metal can survive longer in stagnant areas where the movement of water is restricted.

THE MIGHT OF IMPERIAL ROME IS REFLECTED IN THE FACES OF NOBLE ROMANS FOREVER FROZEN IN STONE. BUSTS LIKE THIS ONE WERE USUALLY CREATED BY GREEK SCULPTORS WHOSE STYLE AND TRADITION WERE ADOPTED BY ROMAN PATRICIANS.

© Scala/Art Resource

teacher, Socrates, and Socrates' great-grandfather, Critias. This conversation included a tale told to Critias by his father that he, in turn, had heard from his own father—all of which may be carrying hearsay a bit far. But Critias reassured the skeptical Socrates that although "the story is a strange one," Solon, regarded as the wisest of Greece's seven wise men, had vouched for it. Solon himself had first heard about Atlantis from Egyptian priests who told him that according to their records the island disappeared under the sea 9,000 years earlier, but that the story hadn't been written down until a thousand years after it had happened. Still, Plato believed every detail of it, and to this day Atlantis is one of the most intriguing of the world's lost civilizations.

Plato's description placed Atlantis in the Atlantic ocean to the west of the Pillars of Heracles, the promontories that flank the strait of Gibraltar. Atlantis was larger, he said, than Asia and Libya combined; in addition, one could easily travel from the European mainland to "the opposite continent" by crossing islands adjacent to it. The Atlanteans connected their cities to the sea with wide canals that were walled and bridged with stone; their buildings were made more beautiful by mixing stone of different colors. The continent's capital city was filled with palaces and temples, including the temple of Poseidon, a structure covered with silver, accented with statues of pure gold, and covered with a roof made of ivory and decorated with gold and silver (metals that were abundant on the island). Plato noted that the building was "somewhat outlandish," but after all, tastes do change in 9,000 years. The stone walls around the city were covered with brass and tin plates—not for added protection, but for added beauty. Their land was productive, providing Atlanteans with every crop they needed as well as "every kind of animal wild and domesticated"; in addition, the marketplace attracted merchants from all corners of the world who, says Plato, "kept up a multitudinous sound of human voices and din and clatter of all sorts night and day."

Although the harbors of Atlantis may have been busy and noisy, the inner regions of the idyllic island were serene, as they were protected from the sea on all sides by high cliffs. The main city was in the center of a flat plain enclosed within high mountains that sheltered it from the north winds. These mountains were filled with thick forests, lakes, and meadows. The water from the rivers flowing down the mountainsides was captured in an immense ditch surrounding the plain and channeled to the city through canals radiating inward from the edge of the plain. The canals provided irrigation for the crops, allowing the Atlanteans to produce two harvests a year, and were used to keep the city supplied with produce from outlying farms and timber from the forests.

There were nine other cities on the island, each ruled by a king who had absolute authority over his subjects, but who also was bound by an agreement that none should make war on another and that they would defend each other from threats to their autonomy. The Egyptian priests told Solon that these kings had conquered most of northern Africa and parts of Europe and would have taken both Egypt and Athens too, but for the bravery of the Hellenes who defeated them. And why did the Athenians not remember such a victory? According to Plato, the Egyptians told their visitor: "At a later time there were earthquakes and floods of extraordinary violence, and in a single dreadful day and night all your fighting men were swallowed up by the earth, and the island of Atlantis was similarly swallowed up by the sea and vanished."

There are several elements in the Atlantis story that make it seem like pure fiction. If the events Plato describes took place more than 9,000 years earlier, it was at least four millenia before the Nile Valley was settled; and the Libyans didn't emerge until about 1000 B.C. There was no city of Athens that long ago, for that matter. And if the Atlanteans possessed thousands of warships, an organized cavalry, chariots, and bronze weapons and artifacts, they were the only people of the world to have such things. The Egyptian priests who were the source of the story had an answer for all that when they told Solon, "You Greeks are all children. . . . You have no belief rooted in old tradition and no knowledge hoary with age." They went on to explain that,

© Susanna Pashko/Envision

"There is at long intervals a variation in the course of heavenly bodies and a consequent widespread destruction by fire of things on the earth. On such occasions, those who live in the mountains or in high and dry places suffer more than those living near rivers or by the sea. . . . When the gods purge the earth with a deluge, the herdsmen and shepherds escape but those living in the cities in your part of the world are swept into the sea by the rivers. [Such events] spare none but the unlettered and the uncultured and you have to begin again like children in complete ignorance of what happened in early times." Today we have much more than just written records to rely on for such information and Solon's story still doesn't add up. Of course, there is always the possibility that the original addition was wrong.

One theory supporting the existence of Atlantis is that the Egyptian histories were translated from an ancient and as yet undecipherable form of writing known as "Linear A"; in this writing, which originated in the Greek islands, the symbols for one hundred and one thousand were almost identical. This raises the possibility that the destruction

THE ABU SIMBEL TEMPLES WERE CARVED FROM SANDSTONE CLIFFS OVERLOOKING THE NILE UNDER THE DIRECTION OF THE EGYPTIAN PHARAOH RAMESES II BETWEEN 1290 AND 1224 B.C. THESE TEMPLES WERE CUT FROM THE MOUNTAIN AND REASSEMBLED ON HIGHER GROUND IN THE 1960S TO PROTECT THEM FROM THE WATERS OF THE RESERVOIR CREATED BY THE ASWAN DAM.

LANDFILL

Centuries from now, scientists may stumble on clues to our civilization in the form of the things we consider garbage. When they do, they'll be following a precedent that began in the 1770s in Egypt when farmers unearthed an ancient landfill and found a cache of discarded statuary and pottery, which they were able to sell to eager collectors. The former dump also produced hundreds of papyrus scrolls, but the farmers weren't so anxious to sell them because they had discovered that when the papyrus was burned it was more aromatic than the finest incense. Nearly all of the scrolls had smoldered away before one, a manuscript in Greek, found its way to Europe and created a stir among scholars. For the next century, similar scrolls, all of them found buried deep in landfills, were exported, but it was a random enterprise that, although intriguing, didn't add as much to the story of ancient Egypt as researchers had hoped. Then, in 1877, an unusually large dumping site, believed to have been the last resting place of the municipal records of the city of Arsinoe, yielded the biggest collection of papyrus scrolls found up to that point. The natives who found them also discovered that there was a lucrative market for them among the Europeans. A decade later, a scientific expedition sent from England specifically to find more scrolls discovered that parts of esophagi were constructed of papier mâché, which undertakers routinely made from whatever waste paper happened to be at hand. By peeling away layers, they found old texts, usually related to each other because they had come from the same wastebaskets. They also found that embalmers preparing sacred animals for burial usually stuffed the carcasses with papyrus scrolls that stayed quite well preserved through the ages. The search of undisturbed garbage heaps in otherwise leveled towns turned up thousands of baskets of scrolls retrieved from the ancient trash, including part of St. Matthew's Gospel copied in the third century. They also found, written on the back of a discarded land surveyor's record, a collection of quotations transcribed in about A.D. 240 that begins with the statement "These are the words which Jesus the living lord spake."

THE SPRAWLING TEMPLES OF KARNAK (OPPOSITE PAGE) IN THE ANCIENT EGYPTIAN CITY OF THEBES WERE BUILT DURING WHAT IS KNOWN AS THE NEW KINGDOM. THE FIRST TO BE BUILT WAS THE TEMPLE OF AMON, BEGUN IN 1490 B.C., AND THE LAST WAS AN UNFINISHED ENTRANCE PYLON ERECTED NEARLY SIX HUNDRED YEARS LATER.

of Atlantis may actually have taken place around 1300 B.C. Another theory is that the Egyptian year was based on thirty-day lunar cycles, which would move the Atlantis legend forward in time to about 1200 B.C., the beginning of a rather catastrophic century. Ancient Egyptian texts say that during the reign of the Merneptah, which began in 1232 B.C., "Libya became a desert; a terrible torch hurled flame from heaven." Another inscription reports that the Nile itself dried up at about the same time. The "terrible torch" is described as a "circling star which spread out his fire in flames." Another inscription reports that "The star of Anat has fallen from heaven; he slew the people of the Syrian land." Similar reports have been unearthed in other parts of the world, and they all agree that in the thirteenth century B.C., the earth was plagued with droughts, earthquakes, floods, tidal waves, and volcanic eruptions. Among the latter, the collapse in approxi-

mately 1220 B.C. of the volcano Thera on the Greek island now called Santorini, has been estimated as ten times more destructive than the 1883 explosion of Krakatoa in Indonesia, which completely destroyed its 2,640-foot (805m) cone and blasted a hole in the ocean floor 1,000 feet (305m) deep. Krakatoa's ash circled the entire world, causing summertime frost and snow on the East Coast of North America nearly a year later; the resulting tidal waves caused destruction as far away as England.

Even if there is no dispute that natural forces can cause a whole continent to disappear, the fate of Atlantis—indeed, its very existence—is still very much in question. The problem, apart from the fact that this landmass is probably under the sea, lies in deciding which sea conceals the lost continent's secrets. Plato placed it in the Atlantic, and some who followed his directions were convinced that the Azores and the Canary Islands are the tops of Atlantean mountains. Others are certain that the lost continent, having been destroyed by Thera's eruption, is in the Aegean. The Bible tells of the land of Ophir, thought to have been in the Indian Ocean, which was the source of the fabled treasure of King Solomon; there have been many claims that Ophir and Atlantis are one and the same. Farther east, the Polynesians also tell of an island empire called Mu that vanished beneath the Pacific. In the 1950s, an underwater search in the North Sea found multicolored stone walls similar to the ones Plato had described; twenty years later, Russian oceanographers managed to photograph a man-made wall 10,000 feet (3,050m) under the Atlantic, west of Gibraltar.

Other theories hold that Atlantis isn't under the sea at all, but is covered by the shifting sands of the Sahara Desert or the thick ice of Antarctica. And in the last half-century hundreds of people have reported seeing what seem to be ancient walls and roads in the part of the western Atlantic known as the Bermuda Triangle. Nearly all of the sightings have been from the air, but some underwater probes have suggested that there is an immense pyramid more than 750 feet (200m) under the sea near the Bahama Banks. Some people, who say that this and

© Shattil-Rozinski/Tom Stack and Associates

no other is the last resting place of the Atlantean civilization, claim that mysterious crystals that were used by the ancients as an energy source are still radiating an electromagnetic force powerful enough to make compasses spin wildly, to black out radar, and to cause electrical failure in engines. This would explain the bizarre disappearances of hundreds of ships and planes in the area. And to add spice to the speculation, the clairvoyant Edgar Cayce prophesied in 1940 that a portion of the Temple of Poseidon would soon be discovered near Bimini and that the first portions of Atlantis would rise again. "Expect it in '68 or '69," he said. The world is still waiting. In the meantime, other lost civilizations have been giving up secrets as fascinating as any that might surface with the lost land of Atlantis.

Chapter 1

Get It In Writing

The Civilizations of the Ancient Near East

The debate is still raging over whether humankind originated in Africa, Asia, or Europe, or simultaneously in all three. There is no question that all the races in the modern world are of the same species, and that wherever it all began, our ancestors started wandering around the earth during the last ice age,

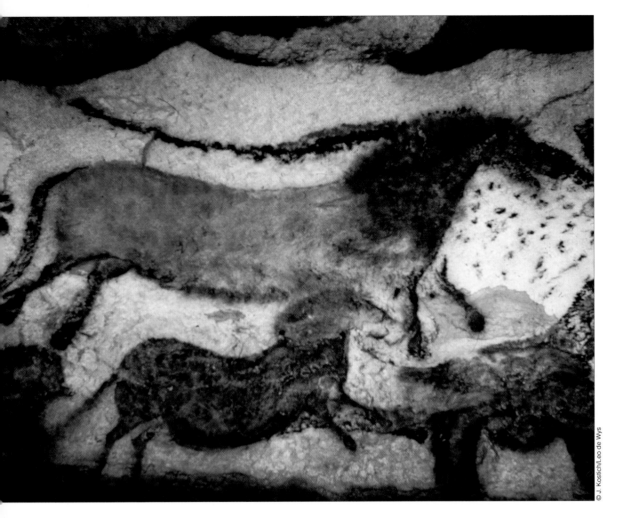

© J. Kostich/Leo de Wys

SUMER

The first of these communities to leave a written record of itself sprang to life in the Tigris-Euphrates Valley of Mesopotamia, in what is now southern Iraq, some 6,000 years ago. It is generally agreed that the Sumerians created one of the world's first civilizations, and their own histories say that their original knowledge came from the gods, who were their ancestors. There is no mention of previous cultures, but it would be foolish to suggest that there hadn't been any, considering that the Sumerians themselves were forgotten for thousands of years.

The first archaeological exploration of Mesopotamia began in the twelfth century, when huge piles of broken tablets were found in the north. It wasn't until more than six hundred years later, however, that it became apparent that the wedge-shaped decorations on the tablets were some sort of written record, and it wasn't until 1850 that anyone discovered where they came from. The breakthrough came when Henry Loftus and Harry Churchill, a pair of British explorers, dug a clay pot from a ruin near the head of the Persian Gulf and found the word "Erech" inscribed on it. The Bible had mentioned such a place, along with other cities with names like Ellasar, Eridu, and Ur, the birthplace of the prophet Abraham. Until that day in the mid-nineteenth century, there had been no other clue that such places ever really existed. In the years since, many Sumerian cities have been uncovered whose ruins tell the story of a race that may have invented the wheel and made bricks and pottery from clay. They apparently were the first to develop irrigation canals to make the desert bloom; in addition they created the first practical plow, a device that also automatically planted seeds. They also seem to have constructed the first sailboats, driven the first chariots, and built the first cities with arches and domes. Of all of their accomplishments, the Sumerians' greatest legacy was the invention of writing.

With the invention of a written language came another first in the history of man's development: the invention of schools. Among the artifacts found

about 100,000 years ago. As they wandered, they changed their ways, creating new tools, new kinds of shelter, and even new social structures to suit the climate and geography of their new surroundings. Cave paintings and sculpture found in France and Spain as well as Africa are at least 30,000 years old, and fossils found in Iraq and China suggest religious rituals and the cultivation of medicinal plants occurring some 500,000 years ago. But it wasn't until about 10,000 B.C. that humans experienced a technological revolution that included the development of cloth and pottery, the cultivation of food crops, and the domestication of animals. These made it easier for prehistoric people to stop wandering and settle down to raise larger families and populate stationary communities. Humankind could start doing things other than just finding food and shelter; the human race was poised on the brink of what we now call civilization.

in the cities of Sumer are hundreds of thousands of tablets containing word lists and exercises that seem to have been used to teach the young to read and write as far back as 3000 B.C. Many of these tablets are also filled with the students' essays, which indicate that the children of the ancients were much like the children of today. In one of these essays a boy reports that he was late for school because his mother didn't have his lunch ready when it was time for him to leave home. The same student also writes that his teacher whipped him for talking in class.

In another essay, a father asks his son, "Where did you go?" and is given the age-old answer "I did not go anywhere." In the exchange that follows, the boy is told to start behaving like an adult. "You who wander about in the public square, would you achieve success?" the father asks. "Perverse one over whom I stand watch, I spoke to my kin, compared its men, but found none like you among them." The rest is quite familiar to any boy who has ever had a long talk with his father, except that this particular conversation took place more than 4,000 years ago. The boy is told to emulate his less rebellious friend, his older brother, even his younger brother, because, his father tells him, "I am tortured because of you. Night and day you waste in pleasure." The ancient trip to the woodshed ends with the warning that, "Your kin waits expectantly for your misfortune, and will rejoice at it because you looked not to your humanity."

The invention of writing also gave the world its first lawyers. Thousands of the surviving Sumerian clay tablets are contracts, wills, deeds, and law codes, all carefully written in the ancient version of the kind of legalese still popular in today's courts of law. The oldest set of written laws yet found, promulgated by the king of Ur in about 2050 B.C., curbed tax collection (which may be another Sumerian invention) and guaranteed that "the widow did not fall prey to the powerful, the orphan did not fall prey to the wealthy." This legal code represented an early manifestation of civil rights legislation; the king wrote that these reforms were being made in the interest of "amargi," a word that translates as "return to the mother."

Although the king's power was absolute in the Sumerian city-states, the people had a voice in the affairs of the government. They had courts of law to settle disputes, and each city had its own elected representatives who met to change laws they considered unfair or to challenge a king who might be overstepping his authority. The first such council dates back as far as 3000 B.C. when the elders of the city of Erech met with representatives of men who could bear arms to decide whether to allow their king to make war on the bigger and more powerful city of Kish.

The war in question was just one of hundreds that had reduced the Sumerians to insignificance by the time the warrior Hammurabi conquered the city of Babylon in the eighteenth century B.C. and turned it into the new center of the Near East. Hammurabi was a leader of the Amorites, a Semitic tribe from the north, and when he merged all the city-states of Sumer into a united kingdom, his language became the official tongue for business and law while the Sumerian language was kept alive for religious purposes and eventually was understood only by priests and scribes. The most significant contribution Hammurabi made was the establishment of a single code of law for his whole empire. The Sumerians had stressed freedom in their laws, but the key facet of the new order was justice, for which Hammurabi used a word meaning "the straight thing."

© Giraudon/Art Resource

© Richard Nowitz/FPG International

EGYPT

If the Sumerians created civilization in the Near East and the Semites improved on it, they weren't alone in their endeavors. At about the same time that cities were rising in the valleys of the Tigris and Euphrates rivers, farmers were migrating from the dry highlands of the northern coasts of Africa and from the deserts of Palestine, Syria, and Libya to the marshes of the upper valley of the Nile. Some time after 4000 B.C. these settlers began draining the swamps to create farms. Although these people apparently developed their civilization independently, there is evidence of Mesopotamian influence in such fields as brick making and boat building, not to mention writing. But with or without any outside help, the Egyptians came together in city-states and were unified under their first king, Menes, in about 3100 B.C.

In the burial places of their kings, the inhabitants of the so-called Old Kingdom of Egypt, which lasted for about four hundred years, left behind vivid descriptions of everyday life that were much more complete than what was included in contemporary Sumerian clay tablet inscriptions. Residential buildings made of mud bricks have long since vanished, but the tombs and temples, which were made of stone, survived. The earliest such tomb was a 204-foot (62m) stepped pyramid built near Memphis in 2700 B.C. This construction started a trend that led in less than a generation to the building of the pyramids of Giza, which were made of immense stone blocks faced with a smooth limestone exterior. The biggest of them, built within a hundred years of

the first, was the pyramid of Khufu (or Cheops), a 481-foot (147m) structure that used six million tons (5.4 million t) of stone. Although the Sumerians had discovered the convenience of wheels by then, the Egyptians hadn't stumbled on the idea yet, and all of the stone blocks were transported to the edge of the desert with sledges and rollers.

The decorations in the royal tombs are reminders of the earthly accomplishments of the dead men buried within. From these descriptions we know that from the earliest times, Egyptian kings sent expeditions to the Sinai for turquoise and copper, and to the heart of Africa for ivory and other treasures. We also know that although slavery existed in the Sumerian cities, it was virtually unknown to the earliest Egyptians. Nearly all of the Egyptian peasants were serfs, however, and paid

WONDERFUL THINGS

The tomb, which added nothing to what was already known about ancient Egypt, had no written documents apart from inscriptions that were almost common cliches by the time it was opened in 1922. It was the last resting place of a minor pharaoh who died at the age of eighteen and whose reign wasn't noted for any out-of-the-ordinary accomplishments. Yet nearly thirty-three centuries after he died, Tutankhamen's name became a household word in countries that didn't exist when he ruled what he had considered the very center of the universe.

When the tomb was first entered by Howard Carter, a draftsman turned archaeologist, his mentor, Lord Carnarvon, was in the passageway behind. "Can you see anything?" asked Carnarvon. "Yes," came the reply, "wonderful things!" As far as world opinion was concerned, this was an understatement, and if the world was not yet interested in ancient history, the beautiful things in what they began calling King Tut's tomb were easy for anyone to appreciate for their contribution to the world of art. The discovery also made the world aware of the science of archaeology as almost no other discovery ever has. Howard Carter was one of a new breed of professionals whose methods were as fascinating as his discoveries. Thanks to him, what had formerly been considered a rich man's hobby (and an eccentricity at best) became not only a recognized profession, but the stuff of high adventure.

The search for Tutankhamen began when a U.S. Egyptologist sold his official permit to explore the Valley of the Kings to Lord Carnarvon after he decided that all the tombs of the pharaohs were empty and not worth the trouble. Although the valley was littered with sand and stones dumped from earlier excavations, Carter himself was not convinced, and he took on the job of proving the American wrong. Not long after he began in 1917, Carter discovered a worker's village near the entrance of the tomb of Ramses VI, but be-

cause the site had already become a major tourist attraction, he opted to look elsewhere. After spending six seasons moving tons of sand and dirt, he went back to the Ramses tomb; four days into their dig his workmen uncovered a stairway cut into the rock. Carter waited three weeks for Lord Carnarvon to arrive from England and together they climbed down the stairs where they found a door with its original seals still intact. Beyond it, through a rubble-filled passageway, another door with the royal seal of the boy pharaoh was all that stood between them and the only intact tomb of an Egyptian king ever found. The first room they entered was filled with the pharaoh's wardrobe and other mementos of his earthly existence. Beyond that was yet another door guarded by gilded statues of sentries. Opening the door to the tomb itself was, Carter said, "the day of days . . . the most wonderful I have ever lived through." Inside the burial chamber, they found four shrines nested together surrounding a sarcophagus containing three coffins, the innermost, made of more than a ton (0.9t) of solid gold, containing the mummy of Tutankhamen himself studded with 143 jeweled ornaments.

Carter spent the next ten years painstakingly cataloging every object in the three rooms that made up the tomb, and everything was photographed in place by an expert from the Metropolitan Museum of Art in New York. Each piece was then crated and moved outdoors to be loaded onto railroad cars to be taken to the Nile, nearly six miles (9.6km) away, on the first leg of their journey to the Egyptian Museum in Cairo. There was no railroad between the valley and the river, however, and only a few sections of track were available to build one. This problem was solved by picking up the iron rails once the train had passed over them and relaying them in front to allow each of dozens of loads of treasure to inch forward toward its faraway destination.

THE PHARAOHS OF EGYPT'S FOURTH DYNASTY (2600–2480 B.C.), KHUFU, KHAFRA, AND MENKAURA, BUILT THE PYRAMIDS AT GIZA (LEFT) TO PROTECT THEIR ROYAL REMAINS THROUGHOUT ETERNITY. THE GIANT PYRAMIDS ARE SURROUNDED BY LESSER TOMBS BUILT FOR THEIR WIVES, AND BY THE TOMBS OF COURT DIGNITARIES. THE MASSIVE STATUE OF PHARAOH AMENHOTEP II (1450–1425 B.C.) AT THE TEMPLE OF KARNAK (BELOW) SHOWS HIM IN CEREMONIAL DRESS WITH A FALSE BEARD AND THE *NEMES*, A STRIPED LINEN HEADDRESS ADORNED AT THE FOREHEAD WITH THE *URAEUS*, THE SACRED ASP, A SYMBOL OF DIVINE POWER.

THE TEMPLE OF AMON (RIGHT, TOP) WAS THE CENTERPIECE OF KARNAK, ONE OF TWO GREAT COMPLEXES ON THE NILE'S EAST BANK AT THEBES. THE NORTHERN PORTION OF KARNAK WAS CONNECTED TO AMON'S SOUTHERN HAREM, LUXOR, BY A CEREMONIAL AVENUE EXTENDING BETWEEN LINES OF RAM'S-HEAD SPHINXES. WHEN THE DECORATION (RIGHT, BOTTOM) OF AN EGYPTIAN TEMPLE OR TOMB WAS FINISHED, PRIESTS INVOKED SECRET MAGIC BELIEVED TO BRING THE FIGURES TO LIFE FOR ALL ETERNITY. IN THE EARLIEST EXAMPLES OF SUCH TOMB ART, FULL FIGURES WERE NOT USED BECAUSE IT WAS BELIEVED THAT IF FINISHED THESE FIGURES MIGHT HARM THE DEAD. THE HUGE GATEWAY (FAR RIGHT) IN FRONT OF THE TEMPLE OF KHONSU AT THEBES WAS BUILT A FEW YEARS BEFORE ALEXANDER THE GREAT CONQUERED EGYPT. THE GATEWAY WAS LATER DECORATED BY PTOLEMY III WHO, THOUGH GREEK HIMSELF, OBSERVED THE LOCAL RELIGIOUS AND ARTISTIC TRADITIONS FOR THE SAKE OF POLITICAL HARMONY.

onerous taxes for the right to produce the food that essentially sustained the kingdom. In fact, heavy taxes are most often blamed for the fall of the Old Kingdom. It is no surprise that in the period of anarchy that followed the Old Kingdom's decline, people began robbing the tombs of the dead kings, the nobles began questioning royal claims of divinity, and local lords took control of individual cities at the expense of the state. Just when it was beginning to seem as though the culture itself would disappear, the kings of the Eleventh Dynasty, headquartered at Thebes, united the civilization again in about 2000 B.C. For the most part, Egypt continued in the same direction it had been following when the period of unrest began, but the scale was different.

Buildings were smaller and pyramids went out of fashion, although sculpture and painting became more sophisticated and widespread. The pharaohs of the new, Middle Kingdom also extended trade farther beyond their borders and welcomed immigrants from such places as Syria and Palestine.

Around this time a series of invasions began, led by warlike peoples thriving in the region. The first of these invaders were the Semites, who probably originated on the Arabian peninsula and, after the domestication of donkeys and camels, became nomadic traders. In their wanderings they came in contact with the new city-states, but they weren't impressed by the idea that people should live together in tight communities tied to the land and to local rulers. They themselves were organized in tribal groups with elected chiefs; the way they saw it, these new societies were fit only to be conquered. They also conquered the Sumerians, bringing a new practice to the civilized world: empire-building. The patchwork empire of the Semites was far from secure, however; the tribes from the mountains to the north and the plains to the east (collectively classified as "Indo-Europeans") comprised the next wave of invaders. The Near Eastern civilizations regarded these tribes as uncultured, uncouth barbarians; by 1700 B.C. the barbarian hordes had destroyed both Hammurabi's Babylonian Empire and Egypt's Middle Kingdom. Interestingly enough, this didn't spell the end of civilization in the Near East; instead, these invasions revitalized the region.

The new city of Ashur (Assur), located near the headwaters of the Tigris River and out of range of the nomadic raiders, eventually became the heart of the great Assyrian Empire. The Assyrians, along with the Hurrians, who probably migrated down from Armenia to the Euphrates valley, carried the remnants of Babylonian culture to the Hittites of Asia Minor and to the Hebrews in Israel. At the same time, Syria was established on the Mediterranean coast and became the center of trade between the inland valleys and all the lands beyond. The new international trade turned out to be one of the greatest civilizing forces in 1500 years.

For Egypt, the Syrian ascendency and the resulting increase in commerce was accompanied by foreign domination. During a period of more than a century, the Nile Delta was ruled by what ancient histories call the Hyksos, probably a Semitic people, who showed Sumerian influences and taught the Egyptians to use wheeled, horse-drawn chariots and to fight with bows and arrows and bronze swords. The advances in the art of war gave the Pharaoh Ahmose the means to drive the Hyksos rulers out and to give his successors a taste for creating an empire of their own.

The Egyptians first expanded southward into Nubia and then marched north through Israel and Syria. Their expanded influence made the Egyptian pharaohs the richest rulers the world had ever seen,

THESE STATUES OF RAMSES II (LEFT, TOP) AT THE ENTRANCE TO THE TEMPLE OF ABU SIMBEL ARE MORE THAN SIXTY-FIVE FEET (19.8M) TALL, CARVED FROM THE FACE OF A CLIFF. THE ENTRANCE WAS ORIENTED SO THAT THE LIGHT OF THE RISING SUN AT THE EQUINOX PENETRATED DEEP INTO THE INTERIOR AND GAVE A MOMENTARY MYSTERIOUS GLOW TO STATUES OF THE GODS INSIDE. RAMSES II, WHO RULED FOR FORTY-SIX YEARS IN THE TWELFTH CENTURY B.C. BUILT MORE THAN HALF THE EXISTING TEMPLES IN EGYPT.

THE SPHINX AT GIZA (LEFT, BOTTOM), 240 FEET (73.2M) LONG AND 66 FEET (20.1M) HIGH, IS CARVED FROM A NATURAL SANDSTONE OUTCROP. ALTHOUGH IT WAS CLEARED IN 1926, THE GUARDIAN OF THE PYRAMIDS WAS BURIED UP TO ITS NECK IN SAND FOR ALMOST 4,500 YEARS.

and they made it a point to lavish their riches on themselves by building palaces and houses for the nobility that were more splendid than any their predecessors had dreamed possible. They also remembered the gods who had made it all possible, especially Amen, whose temple at Karnak is still one of the most impressive monuments of any civilization. They built memorials to themselves, too, like the temple created in the cliffs of the Nile valley by Queen Hatshepsut for the people to worship her memory and the memory of her father Thutmose I. In the desert beyond, other rulers built opulent underground tombs in what became known as the Valley of the Kings, hidden away, they hoped, from grave robbers of the sort who had looted the pyramids of their ancestors.

Akhenaten longed for, however, led to the loss of his empire in Asia. Within a century or two, new attacks from foreign warriors armed with iron weapons wiped out most of the surrounding old Near Eastern kingdoms. By 1200 B.C. only Egypt and Assyria still existed, and neither of them would be able to contemplate expanding beyond their borders for a long time to come.

The Near East's dark age was far from black; it was a time of soul-searching that led to the flowering of the Greek city-states, the refinement of the arts as far away as China, and the beginning of an era when the thinkers Confucius and Buddha, the Hebrew prophets, and the Greek philosophers were all giving humanity new ideas to ponder.

One of the most probed of all mankind's lost civilizations is that of the ancient Israelites. Since its creation in 1948, the modern nation of Israel has been searching for clues to its past; in the process some of the oldest known evidence of agriculture and town life has been found, in the southern corner of the Fertile Crescent. The region was probably settled around the third millenium B.C., and the Hebrews arrived on the scene about a thousand years later.

The Hebrews who settled in Israel had brief periods of glory under kings David and Solomon, but in general had no patience for kings. Instead, the Hebrews developed a political system that was as different from all its predecessors as was the new religion that was at the heart of it. The concept of individual responsibility to a single god made that deity a sterner master than any king could be. While this political and religious system put the Hebrews outside the cultural mainstream, their land was always a coveted prize. The Israelites were overrun by Persians, Babylonians, and Greeks before emerging as an independent kingdom in 168 B.C. One hundred years later the Romans began persecuting the Hebrews and eventually took their land and renamed it Palestine. Through all of these trials the Israelites and their religion survived and incidentally provided posterity with one of the greatest written histories of an ancient people: the Old Testament.

© Van Phillips/Leo de Wys

WHEN KING TUTANKHAMEN'S BODY WAS PREPARED FOR ENTOMBMENT, HIS INTERNAL ORGANS WERE PLACED IN THIS WOODEN CHEST, WHICH WAS COVERED WITH GOLD OVERLAY AND SURROUNDED BY FOUR GOLDEN GODDESSES. THE CHEST, ALONG WITH MOST OF THE TREASURES FROM THE TOMB, IS NOW IN THE CAIRO MUSEUM.

Many of the tombs in the valley were built to honor great generals and some to give enhanced status to certain priests, all of which weakened the pharaoh's claim to godlike status. This trend was broken by Amenhotep IV, who strove to create greater prosperity and a more centralized government. He reformed the government, curbed the power of the priests and generals, and replaced the war god as the central deity with the more benign Aten, the god of the sun. To make the break complete, he changed his name to Akhenaten, "it pleases Aten," and moved his capital more than 300 miles (480km) north of the old one. The peace

THE COLONNADED FORECOURT OF THE TEMPLE OF RAMSES III AT KARNAK IS FLANKED BY ROWS OF STATUES OF THE KING DRESSED AS OSIRIS AND CARRYING THE SYMBOLIC CROOK AND FLAIL. THE CROOK IS A HIEROGLYPH MEANING "RULER," BUT THE SIGNIFICANCE OF THE FLAIL IS UNKNOWN.

Glory and Grandeur

The Mediterranean Civilizations

In the second millenium B.C., as the cultures of the Near East were beginning to feel the winds of change brought by newcomers from the north and east, a new civilization, the Minoan, was flourishing on the island of Crete at the edge of the Mediterranean. Its emergence marked the beginning of a new

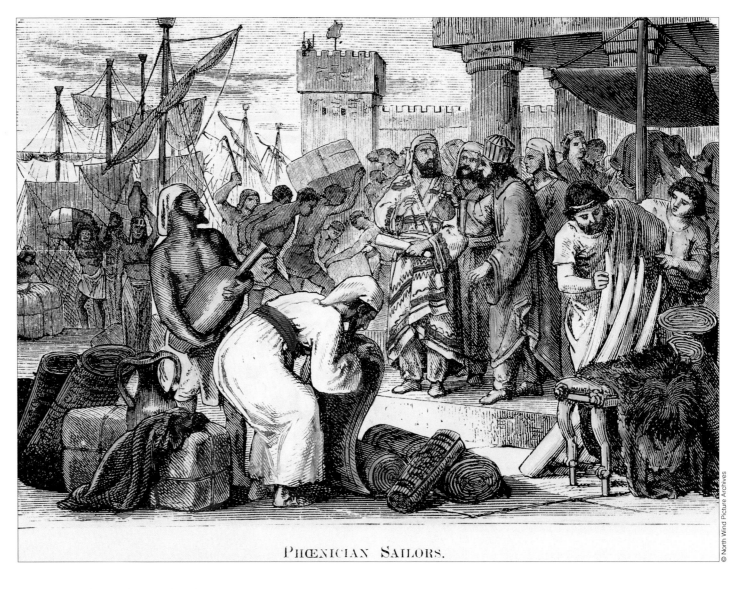

PHŒNICIAN SAILORS.

EVEN IN ITS RUINED STATE, THE PARTHENON (PAGE 26), ON THE ACROPOLIS AT ATHENS, IS STILL INSPIRING. THE MARBLE TEMPLE, WHICH WAS FINISHED IN 432 B.C., WAS BUILT TO HONOR ATHENA. DEVELOPED BY THE ARCHITECT IKTINOS, THE BUILDING CONTAINED A MASSIVE GOLD AND IVORY STATUE OF THE GODDESS.

WHEN NEW YORK'S METROPOLITAN MUSEUM OF ART PAID ONE MILLION DOLLARS FOR THIS GREEK *KRATER* (PREVIOUS PAGE), SIGNED BY THE MASTER ARTIST EUPHRONIOS AND THE POTTER EUXITHEOS, CHARGES WERE LEVELED, BUT NOT PROVEN, THAT IT HAD BEEN STOLEN FROM AN ARCHAEOLOGICAL SITE. ITS AUTHENTICITY, HOWEVER, WAS NEVER QUESTIONED.

era, characterized by a westward march toward the development of some of the grandest civilizations of the ancient world.

PHOENICIA

When Hammurabi pushed the Sumerians aside and established his empire at Babylon, some of his followers kept heading west and settled along the Mediterranean coast. They called themselves Canaanites, "the red people," the Greeks eventually called them Phoinekes, "the people from the purple land," and they are remembered today as Phoenicians. Although originally desert wanderers, the Phoenicians were transformed by their new environment; the availability of cedar trees along the coast led them to become loggers. In addition, they learned to build and sail large ships in order to get the timber to market. Their chief customers were the Egyptians, and the two cultures began to blend as a result. (When the ancient city of Byblos was unearthed in Lebanon in the 1920s, French archaeologists found gold and silver artifacts engraved with Egyptian designs and messages threatening grave robbers with terrible curses that were written in Egyptian hieroglyphics.)

The early Phoenicians were overrun by foreigners in about 1200 B.C., but the invasion proved to be a stroke of luck. It still isn't known whether the conquerors came overland from the north or across the Mediterranean from the island of Crete. The Phoenicians identified the invaders simply as "Sea People." When the two cultures merged they combined the mercantile skills of the red people with the seafaring skills of the newcomers. Before long the lumber business took a back seat to a thriving trade in more profitable merchandise that could be transported long distances overseas. This improved commerce led to the creation of a new kind of empire, and sparked the world's first industrialized society. The Egyptians had discovered the secret of making glass from sand, but had never advanced beyond making milky, opaque jars. Stealing this secret, the Phoenicians figured out how to make transparent glass and then went a step further by developing glass-blowing techniques to mold it into bottles and vases. Before long, huge factories in the Phoenician cities of Tyre and Sidon were mass-producing everything from glass beads and tiles to cut-glass goblets; in the Mediterranean world, even the common people considered it almost barbaric to drink from clay or metal goblets.

The thing that truly made the Phoenicians rich and famous, however, was a sea snail that lived on the beaches of their homeland. The creature secreted a fluid that turned a beautiful shade of purple when dripped on white wool. Because it took thousands of snails to dye a single piece of cloth, purple wool was very rare and therefore expensive. Consequently, purple robes became as much a sym-

© Fridmar Damm/Leo de Wys

bol of royalty as crown and sceptre, and it eventually became the case that a king or emperor wasn't fully dressed without such finery. Thus, Phoenician ships were welcome in every kingdom of the world and, as long as the snails kept reproducing, the merchants could command a king's ransom for their product. These early capitalists also dealt widely in jewelry carved in ivory or gold and silver, as well as in vases and other luxury items. The merchandise that the Phoenicians sold had to be small enough so that they could pack plenty of it into the holds of their ships and expensive enough to make long sea voyages profitable.

TROY

Even though the Phoenicians owned the seas, getting from one body of water to another was and always had been a tricky business. The markets of Asia were reached by the Black Sea but getting to it from the Aegean meant navigating the Dardanelles, a forty-mile (64km) channel laced with rocks and a fast-moving westward current. Most mariners didn't even bother trying to cross, and instead put their cargoes ashore and portaged them across the peninsula to the quieter waters beyond. This area made a perfect site for a settlement and in about 3000 B.C. the great city of Troy was established at the crossroads.

High mountains in the interior made Troy safe from outsiders and the fertile land made it possible for the Trojans to feed themselves. And because they controlled the overland passage, they were able to make a comfortable living by collecting tolls from passing traders. Their location at the center of international trade also put them in contact with other cultures, from which the Trojans freely borrowed. They were eventually wiped out by foreign invaders, but a new Troy rose from the ruins in about 1800 B.C., this time built by settlers from Greece who brought more new ideas. By the time they were destroyed in an earthquake five hundred years later, the new Trojans had developed a city-state more impressive than any on the Greek mainland across the Aegean.

CRETE

The original Trojans probably came from Asia Minor. Others like them had sailed across the Aegean to the island of Crete, where they established themselves between the Dardanelles and the Nile, a strategic point that proved to be the doorway to the eastern Mediterranean. The culture that developed there thrived for about 1,500 years and became known as Minoan (so named for the legendary King Minos). According to myth, Minos conjured a white bull from the sea, angering Poseidon, who consequently caused Minos' wife to mate with the animal. She conceived a monstrous creature with the body of a man and the head of a bull, known as the Minotaur. The king imprisoned the beast in an elaborate maze, the Labyrinth. Once every nine years, Minos forced the Athenians to send seven young men and seven maidens to be sacrificed to the creature. This chain was broken when Theseus, aided by Minos' daughter, killed the beast and escaped the Labyrinth, taking the princess with him.

In 1901, Sir Arthur Evans, an English gentleman, bought an olive grove at Knossos and began poking around the roots of the trees with his walking stick. Within a few weeks he had diggers at work and before long they uncovered the ruins of an

BY THE BOOK

Thanks to the epics of Homer and other Greek poets, the existence of the ancient city of Troy was never doubted, but during most of the eighteenth and nineteenth centuries, when the search for lost civilizations began in earnest, the Turks who controlled Asia Minor were deeply suspicious of Europeans, and few travelers of any kind dared to venture into Turkey. But there was an exception in the person of Heinrich Schliemann, a self-made millionaire who was single-minded about discovering the Troy of King Priam, Achilles, and the beautiful Helen. The seed had been planted in his mind as a young boy in Germany when his father used to read the *Iliad* and the *Odyssey* to him as bedtime stories. He made up his mind to become as rich as possible so that he could one day rediscover Homer's world for himself.

He began his quest by becoming fluent in no fewer than eighteen languages, including ancient Greek, and eventually went to Russia as the agent for an import/export firm, a business he quickly made his own. Once he had made his huge fortune, he retired at the age of forty-two to get on with what he considered his real purpose in life and, leaving his wife behind in Russia, moved to the United States. While waiting for his divorce to be finalized, he took a vacation trip to Greece and tasted the joy of archaeology with a dig on the Ionian island of Ithaca, after which there was no turning back. When he got to the Turkish mainland, an English expedition already there suggested that he come back the following spring. Since Schliemann had a few loose ends to tie up, he agreed. First on his agenda was to acquire a doctorate in history, which he did in a few months, submitting his own autobiography written in classical Greek as his thesis. In the meantime, he finalized his divorce and found a new bride in the person of a seventeen-year-old Greek girl who could converse with him in the language of her ancestors. Then the determined explorer went back to the Plain of Troy to start looking for traces of those ancestors.

The British scientists were still on the Plain of Troy, but they were divided over whether the dig should take place at Hissarlik, close to the sea, or at Bunarbashi a few miles inland. Schliemann called on Homer to settle the argument. By comparing the poet's descriptions, Schliemann concluded that it could only be Hissarlik. There was, however, a catch. The Englishmen had bought the eastern half of the hill, but the newcomer insisted that Troy lay under the western half that, as luck would have it, belonged to two Turks. Schliemann dug there anyway, and when the owners objected, he bought them off by offering them the stones he was clearing from the surface for a bridge they wanted to build. As soon as they had enough stones, however, the Turks drove him off.

It took a year of wheedling and bribery for Schliemann to convince Turkish officials that he should be allowed to continue, but before granting him permission, the Pasha himself bought the western half of the hill in hopes that any treasure under it would be his. He didn't understand that he wasn't dealing with the average treasure hunter—Schliemann was determined to deny the official any riches. When he discovered a copper pot crammed with what appeared to be gold and silver, Schliemann gave his workers a holiday. "It's my birthday," he said, and sent them home before they could see what he had unearthed. After they'd gone, he continued his probe with a pocket knife, uncovering a cache of shields, knives, and jewelry, including more than nine thousand gold rings and buttons. Before the day was over, all of what Schliemann called "Priam's Treasure" was packed in baskets and sent on its way to Greece right under the nose of the Pasha.

Naturally, the official sued and the amateur archaeologist happily paid a fine for his offense of smuggling. But Schliemann didn't return the artifacts. Instead, he made a cash donation equal to the value of the purloined treasure to the Imperial Museum at Istanbul. The Pasha himself got nothing but a hillside, half of which, to the dismay of future archaeologists, had been stripped away in Schliemann's enthusiasm to follow the words of Homer to find the lost city of Troy. He dug through seven different cities that had been built one on top of the other before concluding that the second from the bottom, forty-five feet down, was the one the Greeks had destroyed. It has since been determined that the city Homer described in the *Iliad* was buried even more deeply, although to Schliemann's credit it was, indeed, under the hill the Turks called Hissarlik.

THE TALL, TWO-HANDLED *AMPHORAS* OF THE GREEKS WERE USED TO STORE OIL AND WINE. ELABORATELY DECORATED VERSIONS WERE USED AS PRESENTATION PIECES AT PUBLIC FESTIVALS. VERY LARGE AMPHORAS WERE SOMETIMES USED IN FUNERALS AND WEDDING CEREMONIES.

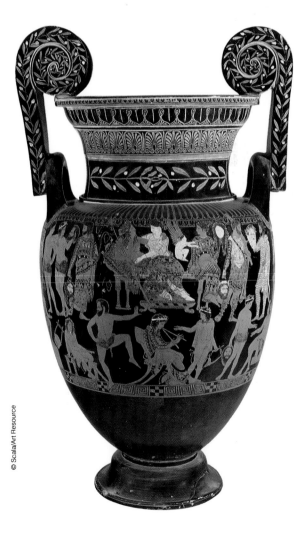

© Scala/Art Resource

STOREROOMS AT THE MINOAN PALACE OF KNOSSOS HELD THE LARGEST COLLECTION OF *PITHOI* (RIGHT), LARGE EARTHENWARE JARS, EVER FOUND. THE ROOMS, BURIED FOR A THOUSAND YEARS, WERE EXPOSED BY AN EARTHQUAKE IN A.D. 67, BUT IGNORED UNTIL 1894 WHEN SIR ARTHUR EVANS EXCAVATED THE PALACE.

THE SPIRAL DECORATION OFTEN FOUND ON POTTERY CREATED IN CRETE, SUCH AS THIS JUG MADE IN ABOUT 180 B.C. (BELOW), IS BELIEVED TO HAVE BEEN INSPIRED BY THE WORK OF EARLY BRONZE AGE POTTERS ON THE CYCLADES ISLANDS IN THE SOUTHEASTERN AEGEAN. THE FRESCO DEPICTING THE BULL GAMES (BELOW, RIGHT) FOUND ON THE WALL OF A COURT AT THE PALACE OF KNOSSOS OFFERED PROOF THAT MEN AS WELL AS WOMEN TOOK PART IN THE DANGEROUS SPORT. IN MINOAN PAINTING, MALE SKIN TONE WAS ALWAYS RED AND FEMALE ALWAYS WHITE.

© Robert Zehring

© Sandak/FPG International

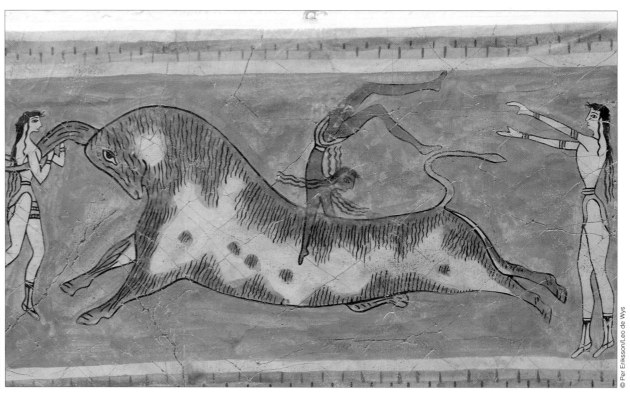

© Per Eriksson/Leo de Wys

ancient palace sprawling over more than five acres (2ha). Evans kept digging for most of the rest of his life and found traces of other palaces and other cities, connected by paved roads and served with aqueducts that supplied water to buildings equipped with indoor plumbing. He even found evidence in frescoes that religious ceremonies involved gymnastic dances with bulls. He concluded that the sprawling palace he found could easily have been a hopeless maze to any stranger because its corridors frequently turned in on themselves and sometimes led nowhere at all. He also discovered that the Minoans were conquered in about 1500 B.C. by the Mycenaeans, descendants of Indo-European tribes that had settled on the Greek Peninsula a few hundred years earlier.

GREECE

The Mycenaeans themselves were overrun in the fateful twelfth century B.C. when northern tribes moved in on the Near Eastern civilizations. Greece was invaded by the Dorians, who swept in over the Balkans, bringing iron with them. For more than two hundred years the Greeks struggled to survive; the advantage of having a common language and historical tradition, in addition to living in a land isolated from the rest of the world, helped them to become a unified people. Ironically it was the Dorians who showed the Greeks how to unite by bringing scattered villages together into city-states that were easier to control. The Greeks fully adopted this idea, as evidenced by Aristotle's statement that "Man is by nature an animal intended to live in cities."

For hundreds of years, the most important city-state was Sparta, established in the southeastern region of Greece as a base for military strikes. It was so powerful that it existed for more than eight centuries without protective walls—simply put, the Spartans were the most dangerous warriors anywhere. Each city-state, which the Greeks called a "polis," was built along similar lines. They were situated on high ground, where floods would not be

THE ACROPOLIS AT ATHENS (LEFT) WAS DEDICATED TO THE GODS, ESPECIALLY ATHENA. IN THE MONTH OF HEKATOMBAION (JULY/AUGUST), ALL ATHENIAN CITIZENS PARTICIPATED IN A PROCESSION PAST THE TEMPLES TO MARK THE GODDESS' BIRTHDAY DURING THE FESTIVAL OF THE PANATHENAIA. THE *THOLOS* AT DELPHI (BELOW) IS A CIRCULAR BUILDING; THIS DESIGN WAS UNCOMMON IN CLASSICAL GREEK ARCHITECTURE.

MOSAIC FLOORS, SUCH AS THIS ONE (ABOVE) DATING FROM THE FIFTH CENTURY B.C. ON THE ISLAND OF RHODES, WERE CREATED BY NEARLY EVERY CULTURE IN THE ANCIENT NEAR AND MIDDLE EAST. WHEN HE EXCAVATED THE GRAVES AT THE CITADEL OF MYCENAE, HEINRICH SCHLIEMANN FOUND THIS SOLID GOLD MASK (OPPOSITE PAGE) AND ANNOUNCED, "I HAVE GAZED ON THE FACE OF AGAMEMNON." SCHOLARS HAVE SINCE DATED THE MASK TO THE SIXTEENTH CENTURY B.C., THREE CENTURIES BEFORE THE BIRTH OF THE CELEBRATED KING.

a problem, and far from the sea, to eliminate the possibility of sudden invasions from abroad. The entire population lived together behind fortifications on level ground at the foot of the acropolis. Citizens of these city-states became fiercely patriotic; leaving one's city was considered criminal, even though the next city was just as Greek as the last. It wasn't uncommon for the citizens of one city-state to swear oaths of everlasting hatred toward the people of another. For centuries, in fact, they fought one another in what can be described as a long and costly family feud.

The tradition of fierce loyalty to a city had its roots in the idea that every citizen was a participating member of the government and not just its subject. Within each city-state, all citizens were (theoretically) equal and had the same rights and responsibilities. Over the centuries, tyrants came and went, but the democratic ideal gave the Greeks security and a sense of order, both of which were important to the average Greek.

Not all the Greeks were in Greece, however. With the help of the Athenians, who were less affected by the Dorian invasions, refugees from Mycenae crossed over to the mainland of Asia Minor and settled in the land they called Ionia. They, too, lived in diverse city-states that were separated by internal politics. While the political structure on the mainland was held together by loyalty to local gods, the

Ionians shared a common religion. It brought them together for athletic contests and music festivals that gave them a chance to recite poetry celebrating the heroes and gods of their ancestors. Other Greeks ranged into southern Italy and Sicily, which was the location of the Corinthian colony of Syracuse. Larger than most of the city-states back home, Syracuse later became the biggest city in Europe. They settled in northern Africa and even along the shore of the Black Sea. The Greeks were already emerging from their dark age, and their colonies helped speed up the enlightenment process. The home states grew rich, but the non-Greek world grew richer still as a new kind of civilization began replacing the old ones.

Contact with the outside world after 750 B.C. changed Greece, too. Greek pottery, which had previously been beautifully decorated with orderly geometric patterns, suddenly began to include figures of animals, flowers, humans, and other natural forms that had been used in the Near East for centuries. The Near Eastern cultures also inspired Greek sculptors to begin expressing themselves in life-size, and larger, representations of both humans and gods. And, inspired by the Egyptians, Greek architects began replacing the simple structures of their ancestors with temples and buildings far more magnificent than anything that had preceded them anywhere in the world. In the centuries that followed, Greek art and architecture kept improving on itself. The Greeks improved on original ideas they borrowed, infusing them with a sense of order and a sense of humanity that almost no other culture, before or after, could match.

As the Greek culture was evolving, Cyrus, the King of Persia, was conquering the Near East. When Egypt fell to his son in 525 B.C., the entire area from the Mediterranean to the Indus Valley and from the Persian Gulf to the Black Sea was swallowed up by the Persian Empire. They also controlled Macedonia and Thrace along the northern Aegean coast and in 490 B.C., they decided to take the rest of the peninsula. The Athenians defeated them on the Plain of Marathon, but ten years later the Persians came back—defeating them

© Robert Zehring

ALL THE MARBLES

In the eighteenth century, the search for lost civilizations was more often than not a search for artifacts to decorate the mansions of the rich. One of England's most avid collectors was Thomas Bruce, the Earl of Elgin. When he became Britain's ambassador to the court of the Sultan of Turkey in 1798 (during an era when the Turks controlled Greece), Bruce found himself on the inside track for securing some of the greatest treasures of antiquity. His position presented an opportunity to further, as he put it, "the progress of the Fine Arts in Britain." He began by securing permission to send a team of Italian artisans to Athens to make plaster casts of ancient Greek sculptures. Their primary target was the city's greatest treasure, the Parthenon, whose pediments were adorned with sculptures of the goddess Athena and whose walls were covered with reliefs and friezes showing both events in the lives of the gods and religious ceremonies of the early Greeks. The temple itself had been severely damaged a century earlier when Venetian raiders scored a direct hit on a powder magazine inside; by the time the artisans arrived to make their plaster copies of what was left, a great deal of the structure had been stripped by local builders who considered it little more than a handy quarry.

In spite of the devastation, the ground was still strewn with artifacts, but before they could be sorted out by the Italian workers, the local governor voided their permit on the grounds that foreigners on the hillside would be spending too much of their time looking down on the Turkish women in the streets below. Lord Elgin took his case to the Sultan himself and managed not only to have the permit restored, but added language that

allowed his people to also take away any pieces of stone bearing inscriptions, "when they wish[ed] to." Dismantling the Parthenon had been the ambassador's fondest wish all along, and in the summer of 1801, a huge crew of laborers began attacking the structure with sledgehammers and crowbars. By the end of the year, every bit of the sculpture from the temple's west pediment was on its way to England; the following year the east pediment was also bared. In the meantime, most of the friezes were removed along with architectural elements from other nearby temples, and all of it hauled away. The rape went on for a full ten years.

All the work was done at Elgin's personal expense, which made him the owner of the sculptures, and he built a special exhibit hall on the lawn of his estate to show them off to a dazzled public back home. Although he had financed the acquisition of a priceless treasure, he had gone broke in the process; furthermore, an attempt to sell the Greek sculptures to the British Museum failed when the trustees refused to pay him more than £30,000 for the lot, about half of what he had spent. Faced with bankruptcy, he was forced to sell his house; he subsequently moved the treasures to the home of a friend. Then, British art historians began whispering that the sculptures were not Greek at all, but copies made by Romans. His spirit broken, Lord Elgin finally accepted the museum's offer and promptly left the country. He left England a priceless piece of antiquity the Greek government has been trying unsuccessfully to recover ever since. The English, who don't deny that the sculptures graced the Parthenon for two thousand years, still insist on calling them the Elgin Marbles.

wasn't so easy the second time. Spartan soldiers, all of whom were killed, delayed the Persian infantry at Thermopylae Pass near their crossing point in the Dardanelles and a Greek fleet turned back the Persian warships, but the invaders kept coming and Athens was evacuated. The leaders of the Greek city-states began arguing among themselves over what to do next. The Athenian admiral Themistocles, who favored attacking the Persian ships in the narrow strait off the island of Samos, settled the argument by threatening to load the entire population of Athens on his ships to start a new city across the Mediterranean. Once he made his point, he sent a spy to the Persian king Xerxes, with word that the Athenians were in a mood to surrender and the suggestion that he should attack before their mood changed. In the sea battle that followed, Xerxes lost more than two hundred ships and the rest of his sailors rowed for their lives back in the direction of Asia Minor. Most of the ships were manned by Ionian mercenaries, who suddenly remembered their Greek roots and revolted. Meanwhile, back in Greece, men who had sworn blood oaths against rival city-states were moved to a new kind of patriotism when the Athenians proclaimed their "common brotherhood with the Greeks...the common character which we bear." The war against the Persians was far from over, but Greece was finally united, at least for a while, and Athens was first among equals.

Even though the city-states were unified, however, they couldn't resist fighting among themselves and

although their culture flourished, their power began to decline. In 339 B.C., Philip, the king of the Macedonians, moved down from the north to claim all Greece as his own. His son, Alexander the Great, went on to invade the Persian Empire, and in five years it was his. By the time his campaign ended, Alexander had extended Hellenistic civilization

THE EXCAVATION OF THE FORTRESS AT MASADA WAS ACCOMPLISHED BY AN ARMY OF VOLUNTEERS. EVERY YEAR, SOME SIX THOUSAND FOREIGNERS, TWO-THIRDS OF THEM WOMEN, SHOW UP IN ISRAEL TO WORK ON SUCH PROJECTS. THERE IS PLENTY FOR THEM TO DO: OF ABOUT FOUR HUNDRED ANCIENT MOUNDS, FEWER THAN SIXTY HAVE GIVEN UP THEIR SECRETS.

© Louis Goldman/FPG International

BACK FROM THE BRINK

One of the very few ancient civilizations that has never been completely lost, despite attempts by other cultures to destroy it, is the one advanced by the Hebrews. When Jerusalem fell to the Romans in A.D. 70 and the Hebrew people were forced to leave their homeland, about a thousand patriots, including women and children, went instead to the top of a flat-topped mountain near the Dead Sea known as Masada. It was a perfect refuge, a fortress 1,700 feet (517m) above the plain that was surrounded by an eighteen-foot (5.5m) wall. A higher walled structure, filled with enough supplies and weapons to serve an army of 10,000, stood inside. The top of the mesa, a half-mile (0.8km) across, was thickly covered with a rich topsoil good for growing food; a system of natural springs and cisterns guaranteed that anyone could survive a siege lasting many years. These displaced individuals called themselves the "Zealots."

The Zealots found themselves under siege almost as soon as they reached the summit. The Roman Tenth Legion, commanded by Flavius Silva, had followed them there from Jerusalem and set up camp on the plain below. His first assault was on the western side, where he had ordered construction of a series of platforms that reached to within 150 feet (45.6m) of the top. With typical Roman determination, Silva topped it off with a square stone pier that became a base for a siege tower equipped with catapults and a battering ram. After all their work, the Romans found that the ram couldn't make more than a small hole in the wall, and that its pounding served only to pack the dirt and rubble behind it into an even harder barrier. Flavius Silva had a backup plan. The outer wall was made of wood, and he simply set fire to it and then he and his men went back down the plain to get a good night's sleep. In the morning, the walls were still burning and the Romans mounted their final attack. It had taken them three years to get to this point and they were more than ready for a

good fight, but instead, when they reached the top, they were greeted by a deathly silence.

The night before, when the walls began to burn, the Zealots gathered together and stiffened their resolve never to be servants of Romans or anyone else except God. They decided to burn all their possessions, except their substantial food supply; leaving the food intact would serve as a testament to the fact that they had not been starved out, but had chosen death over slavery. Ten of them were designated executioners; during that night these men killed the 957 survivors, then held a lottery to kill each other; in the end, only one was left, and he became a suicide. The message was not lost on the Romans who, their historian recorded, "... could only wonder at the courage of their resolution."

After the Romans left, almost no one ever went up to the top of the mountain again, although the Jews of the diaspora never forgot the story of what had happened that night at Masada.

It was proven to be more than just a legend in 1963–64 when five thousand volunteers from twenty-eight countries led by Yigael Yadin, the former chief of staff of the Israeli Army and a professional archaeologist, cleared the mountaintop of some 150,000 cubic yards (114,750kl) of dirt and debris. They found the skeletons of some of the Zealots as well as lamps and jewelry, coins, and even a prayer shawl left untouched for nineteen centuries. They also found the remains of the Roman camp and the ruins of a palace whose mosaics are the oldest ever discovered in the Holy Land. Possibly their most important discovery consisted of fragments of scrolls that had been buried at Masada in A.D. 73.

These were duplicates of scrolls discovered in a cave at Qumran on the shore of the Dead Sea a few years earlier and served to confirm the age and probably the authenticity of the so-called Dead Sea Scrolls.

© Stephen Varone/Photo Network

more than 2,300 miles (3,700km) from Greece into the heart of Asia. Among the most significant changes during Alexander's rule was the building of a new capital in Egypt (one of about seventy-five Asian cities to be named Alexandria), and the establishment of a new ruling dynasty descended from the Macedonian general Ptolemy. The city Alexander had made the most important in Egypt was the last piece of his sprawling Hellenistic empire to fall to Roman conquerors three hundred years later.

ROME

Until the reign of Alexander, not many observers would have bet that the Romans would ever amount to anything. The Greeks dominated southern Italy and Sicily and the north was the undisputed turf of one of the most mysterious of all the lost civilizations, the Etruscan. The remains of their cities and their elaborate tombs show traces of Asian influence, but the Etruscan language, most of which is still indecipherable, seems unrelated to any other, either among Asian or early Italian tribes. Furthermore, no one really knows where the Etruscans came from. Their alphabet was Greek and their art shows Greek influence, which is hardly surprising considering that their neighbors to the south were Greeks. Even though they absorbed foreign ideas, the Etruscans did have imaginations of their own; in fact, some of their neighbors found the Etruscan society positively scandalous. "They have no shame," reported a Greek historian who was shocked to report that Etruscan women not only walked the streets side by side with men, but actually were allowed to recline with them on couches at dinnertime. In addition, the Etruscans were unabashed lovers of pleasure, and later Roman historians suggested that that lack of morals contributed to their disappearance.

While the Etruscans were building cities, creating art, and improving techniques of agriculture, scattered tribes in the center of Italy, the land the Etruscans called Latium, began settling a spot on the Tiber River where an island made it easy to cross from one side to another. The earliest history of Rome is wrapped in legends of heroes and villains, beginning with the city's founding in 753 B.C. by Romulus and Remus, the twin sons of a vestal virgin. The story says that the boys' mother, Rhea Silva, abandoned them to the river when they were born, but that they washed ashore and were adopted by a she-wolf who kept them alive. As adults, they founded the city to honor the gods who had supervised their rescue. A difference of opinion over who should be king led to Remus' murder by Romulus, who became the king and namesake of the settlement overlooking the Tiber. The legends say that other peoples, especially the Sabines, were assimilated by the Romans and that eventually even the Etruscans recognized the Romans' superiority. It is more likely that in about 600 B.C., Rome became an Etruscan city and during the next hundred years developed into a cultural center every bit as important as Athens, which was becoming influential at the same time.

Under its Etruscan kings, Rome also became a strong military power, extending its influence far to the south. The engineering skills of the people from the north not only gave the Romans an architectural tradition of their own, but enabled them to build roads and bridges connecting their city with the rest of Italy. Rome's Etruscan period ended in 509 B.C. and was replaced by the Republic, which after a shaky start conquered all of Italy in about two hundred years. All of Italy, that is, except the Greek-held southern tip. The Greeks hoped to keep their foothold by inviting King Pyrrhus of Epirus to lead an army against the Romans. He won most of the battles and even reached the gates of Rome itself, but the Romans refused to surrender and Pyrrhus eventually retreated, leaving the Greek colonies to be absorbed. The Romans were masters of the entire peninsula, and the rest of the world was put on notice that these upstarts (who could bring Greece's most professional army to its knees) were going to be heard from again.

Like the tough gunslingers of many tales of the Wild West, the Romans were challenged to prove their strength, prompting the historian Edward Gibbon to write that the Romans built their empire through self-defense. Among the early challengers were the Carthaginians, successors to a Phoenician city-state in northern Africa, who controlled trade in the western Mediterranean. When the Carthaginians began expanding in Sicily, the Romans sent an army to check them, but without ships it was an ill-conceived war. The obvious answer was to build vessels of their own, and legend says that using a wrecked Carthaginian warship as a model, the Romans constructed 120 ships in less than two months. They even added a wrinkle of their own: a hooked gangplank that allowed the crew to board enemy ships. In less than a decade, the new Roman navy had subjugated Sicily, Sardinia, and Corsica. Conquering Carthage itself would take a little longer.

Rome declared war on the Carthaginians in 218 B.C. and it took fifteen years of hard fighting, mostly in Italy itself (armies led across the Alps by Hannibal had taken the war all the way to Rome), before Carthage finally fell. The victory gave the Romans control of all the territories Carthage had claimed including Spain, except a narrow strip along the

THE ELABORATE TOMBS OF THE ETRUSCANS, WHOSE CIVILIZATION THRIVED IN ITALY BETWEEN THE EIGHTH AND FIRST CENTURIES B.C., WERE FILLED WITH LUXURIES TO BE USED IN THE AFTERLIFE. SCULPTURES OF THE DECEASED OFTEN HAD OUTSTRETCHED HANDS THAT WERE FILLED WITH REAL FOOD.

coast of North Africa. Some years later the Carthaginians violated their treaty and the Romans attacked again. Before they left, they completely destroyed the city of Carthage, plowed the ruins under the ground, and spread salt over the earth to keep it from rising again. Meanwhile, the citizens of Rhodes and Athens, obviously impressed by Rome's new power, invited the Roman armies to protect them against the king of Macedonia. Success in this matter spurred the Romans on to move farther east and clip the wings of Asian powers with designs on Alexander's empire. The conquered states were allowed to keep their own governments and were organized together under Roman protection, a strategy that had worked well in Italy. By defeating Carthage and the Hellenistic kingdoms, the Romans had set the stage for empire-building on a tremendous scale.

The Romans imposed their way of life on the provinces through their occupying armies and set up governments everywhere that were modeled on their own. They empowered their representatives to collect taxes and both tax collectors and Roman officials grew rich from the bounty. But if the Romans were pleased to force their imperial will on the rest of the world, they were also forced to accept the significant influence of Greek culture on the Roman. This influence had always been strong, but during the early wars in southern Italy, Roman soldiers were impressed by the sophistication of the cities they attacked. They admired the buildings and the art, and they found the food in particular and the lifestyle in general quite superior to what they were familiar with back home. Later, when the Romans penetrated the East, they sent slaves and hostages back to Rome, some of whom were highly

educated Greeks who became teachers and advisors to the Roman patricians. In time, knowledge of the Greek language and an understanding of Greek philosophy became the marks of a truly cultured Roman citizen.

The Greeks influenced every facet of Roman life from politics to literature, but the most visible impact was on the city itself. The basilica, a long narrow building with interior columns dividing a wide central hall from side aisles, which became the standard for Roman public buildings (and eventually for Christian churches), was a Greek structure. The houses of the wealthy Romans all had collonaded central courts called "peristyles," mosaic floors, and wall paintings and sculpture of the kind that made an impression in classical Greece long before the founding of Rome. Roman buildings were often designed by Greek architects and the fine hand of Italian artisans would more often than not be guided by the Greeks. The culture the Greeks themselves had carried to the East was carried westward by the conquering Romans. Like many other vanquished civilizations, Greek civilization had a significant influence on its conquerors.

Of course, this isn't to say that the Romans made no innovations of their own. In the second century B.C., for example, the Romans made the remarkable discovery that sand and lime mixed together with water not only made a good adhesive to hold stones together, but could be used as a building material all by itself. The Greeks themselves had worked with concrete, but in the hands of the Romans it led to the construction of solid arches, domes, and vaults, and led to the creation of long aqueducts and bigger buildings, including their masterpiece, the Pantheon.

Before its decline, the Roman Empire extended over three continents; it was with good reason that its citizens regarded Rome as *caput mundi*, "the capital of the world." Their worldview, however, was fairly limited. Alexander the Great's adventures had made them aware of cultures in India, but they were not aware of an empire very similar to their own that existed in the dark world beyond, a civilization equally if not more accomplished.

First Light in the East

China and the Far East

As the civilizations of the Near East were emerging in the Tigris-Euphrates Valley, another culture was developing in the fertile valley of the Indus River in what is now India and Pakistan. It is believed that the entire region was united as a single state that covered more than 600,000 square miles

(1,554,000 sq km). In the meantime, civilization was also developing even farther to the east, in China; as the Near Eastern cultures looked westward, their counterparts were taking their ideas east and south, spreading into vast new territories.

CHINA

In 221 B.C., at almost exactly the same time that Rome defeated Carthage and began building an empire beyond the Italian peninsula, Prince Cheng of Chin, a thriving state more than 5,000 miles (8,000km) to the east, ended nearly two centuries of fighting by defeating the last of six neighboring countries and declaring himself Chin Shih Huangti, the First Emperor of China. The government he created lasted virtually intact until the early twentieth century, and the territory he began uniting into an empire 2,200 years ago still exists as a single state. Amazingly, the Chin Dynasty itself lasted just fifteen years—possibly the most incredible decade and a half in the history of civilization. Shih Huangti declared his power absolute and, following the tradition of the Chin kings before him, he cut the power of the nobility by appropriating their lands and forcing them to move near his capital at Hsienyang where he could keep an eye on them. He had the empire divided into provinces and ordered that a careful census be taken to make sure everyone paid taxes and to provide a list of possible conscripts for his army or for forced labor. He needed the soldiers to protect his empire, of course, but he also used them to expand his domain down the coast as far as Canton and south into Vietnam.

As it turned out, Shih Huang-ti needed more laborers than soldiers. During his short reign, he began a network of highways that extended from Hsienyang to every corner of his domain. To make these highways even more useful he decreed that the axles of all chariots and carts should be the same width so that the ruts in the roads would be uniform everywhere. Before his time, it had been necessary for travelers to change vehicles from place to place, depending on the wheel-tracks in that region. Shih

PAGE 42: THE 10,000 FIGURES SCULPTED IN THE BUDDHA CRESCENT TOOK MORE THAN 250 YEARS (FROM THE TANG TO THE SONG DYNASTIES) TO COMPLETE. LOCATED IN THE REMOTE DAZU REGION OF CHINA, THIS AND SOME FORTY OTHER SITES WERE UNKNOWN TO THE OUTSIDE WORLD, AND SAFE FROM DESTRUCTION, UNTIL A ROAD WAS BUILT IN 1982. THIS PAGE: THE GREAT WALL OF CHINA, BEGUN WITH SEPARATE SECTIONS DURING THE WARRING STATES PERIOD, ABOUT 403 B.C., ONCE EXTENDED SOME 6,200 MILES (9,982 KM) FROM THE YALU RIVER IN THE NORTHEAST TO XINJIANG IN THE NORTHWEST. THE WATCHTOWERS (RIGHT) PLACED AT REGULAR INTERVALS WERE USED AS BEACON TOWERS.

AFTER CHINA WAS UNIFIED UNDER SHIH-HUANG-TI, A MASSIVE ARMY OF WORKMEN BEGAN WORK ON THE GREAT WALL, WHICH EVENTUALLY INCORPORATED ENOUGH BRICK AND STONE TO BUILD AN EIGHT-FOOT (2.4M) WALL COMPLETELY AROUND THE WORLD. THE WALL'S BADALING SECTION NEAR BEIJING (FAR RIGHT), NOW A TOURIST ATTRACTION, WAS FINISHED DURING THE MING DYNASTY (1368–1644). THE 21.5-FOOT (6.6M) WALL WAS WIDE ENOUGH (18 FEET [5.5M]) TO ACCOMMODATE TEN INFANTRYMEN MARCHING ABREAST. BEGINNING IN THE SIXTH CENTURY, THE GREAT WALL LOST ITS EFFECTIVENESS AGAINST NORTHERN INVADERS, WHO HAD DISCOVERED THEY COULD CROSS THE BARRIER IF THEY WERE GENEROUS IN BRIBING THE SENTRIES. WIND AND WATER EROSION HAVE DESTROYED MANY SECTIONS, BUT EVEN TODAY THE WALL (BELOW, RIGHT) IS 3,750 MILES (6,038 KM) LONG.

Huang-ti also greatly expanded the system of canals to make farms more productive, and decreed that farmers had the right to own their own land, an innovation that made the farmers more productive.

Shih Huang-ti's greatest accomplishment, however, was the construction of a huge wall to guard his empire. One of the first things he did as emperor was to send 300,000 soldiers and peasants to drive the nomadic tribes out of the north and to build a barrier to keep them from coming back. When these laborers were finished, they had connected existing walls and built new ones to form a continuous fortification more than 1,400 miles (2,240km) long. Although it has been altered, extended, and even relocated in the centuries since, the Great Wall is still one of the legacies of China's first emperor, but it isn't the only one. With the help of his chief minister, Li Ssu, one of the greatest legal minds of any era, Shih Huang-ti created a bureaucracy that kept every square foot of the new empire under tight control. And to make sure there was no chance of any uprisings, he ordered all civilians to give up their weapons, which were then melted down to make a dozen giant statues outside his palace.

The first emperor also ordered the burning of all books that glorified the past (although he allowed books on medicine and agriculture as well as the history of the Chins to survive), and kept copies of the banned books in his own imperial library. He also standardized the written language by ordering the creation of new characters to replace the varied script used in different parts of his empire so that everyone who could read would understand what was to be expected of them, in the process providing the foundation for a literary tradition that would enrich the entire Chinese empire.

Accomplishing so much so quickly convinced Shih Huang-ti that he really was the Son of Heaven, which kings before him had claimed to be. To enhance this image, he put 700,000 of his subjects to work building an imperial palace more grand than anything that had previously existed. It took them ten years and the building wasn't completely finished before the emperor died. In the meantime, other workers were kept busy building replicas of

THE TOMB OF EMPEROR SHIH-HUANG-TI, DISCOVERED AT XIAN IN 1974, WAS FILLED WITH CLAY REPLICAS OF HIS HUGE ARMY, INCLUDING THIS KNEELING ARCHER (LEFT), WHICH IS ABOUT FOUR FEET (1.2M) TALL. AT THE TIME THE TOMB WAS SEALED, EACH OF THE FIGURES WAS PAINTED IN BRIGHT COLORS. THE PHANTOM ARMY (BELOW) PROTECTING THE IMPERIAL TOMB HAS BEEN SILENTLY STANDING GUARD OVER THE DEAD EMPEROR FOR MORE THAN TWO THOUSAND YEARS. THE TORSO OF EACH FIGURE IS HOLLOW, AND THE LEGS AND ARMS ARE SOLID. THE FACES WERE SCULPTED FROM MODELS SELECTED FROM THROUGHOUT THE EMPIRE.

THE CLAY ENTOURAGE GUARDING SHIH-HUANG-TI'S TOMB INCLUDES NEARLY SIX THOUSAND INFANTRYMEN STANDING FOUR ABREAST IN ELEVEN PARALLEL TRENCHES. THE INSTALLATION OF THESE FIGURES, KNOWN AS *MINQUI*, "SPIRIT OBJECTS," REPLACED THE FUNERARY PRACTICE OF HUMAN SACRIFICE FOR THE FIRST TIME UNDER SHIH-HUANG-TI.

the palaces of the rulers of states conquered by the Chin, all of them connected by underground passages so the emperor could move from one to the other when he wanted a change of scene.

Although Shih Huang-ti may have thought he was the Son of Heaven, he knew he wasn't immortal and throughout his entire reign work was carried on to construct an elaborate underground tomb where he would spend eternity. It was reported to have been built with a bronze floor and lacquered walls and contained models of all of the major buildings he had built as well as a relief map of his empire that included rivers and oceans filled with mercury. The ceiling, a map of the heavens, was studded with pearls representing stars. The historical record says that "Rare objects and costly jewels were collected from the palaces and from the various officials and stored in vast quantities."

To make sure that the treasures stayed buried, mechanical crossbows set to release a rain of arrows were concealed in the entrances; to make sure the tomb stayed hidden, the workmen who set the traps and filled the treasure rooms were all buried alive with their dead emperor. Trees and grass were

THE CARVING OF FIGURES OF BUDDHA (LEFT) AROUND THE LONGMEN CAVES, LOCATED ALONG THE YI RIVER NEAR LUOYANG, BEGAN IN A.D. 494 AND CONTINUED INTO THE SEVENTH CENTURY. ACCORDING TO LEGEND, THE BUDDHIST SUTRAS WERE INTRODUCED TO CHINA NEAR THESE CAVES FROM INDIA IN A.D. 68 BY TWO MONKS RIDING ON A WHITE HORSE. THE 1,300 LONGMEN CAVES (BELOW), ALSO KNOWN AS THE DRAGON CAVES, CONTAIN MORE THAN 2,100 GROTTOES, SEVERAL PAGODAS, AND AN ESTIMATED 100,000 IMAGES AND STATUES OF BUDDHA. THE HARD ROCK MADE FINE CARVING POSSIBLE, AND IT IS SAID THAT MORE THAN 800,000 ARTISANS TOOK PART IN THE WORK.

THE VERDICT OF HISTORY

Shih Huang-ti, the first emperor of China, was one of the most remarkable men in the history of civilization. He united the warring states and created a political system that endured for 2,200 years—longer than any other. But history has not been kind to him. Not long after he died, the scholar Jia Yi wrote an essay called "The Sins of Chin," in which he charged that the emperor "cracked his great whip to bend the world to his will [and] placed deceit and violence above kindness and justice, making tyranny the foundation of his empire." The fact that the so-called tyrant had burned all the books written before his time that he considered offensive and had had scholars buried alive may have had something to do with it, but all future Chinese historians made a point to paint Shih Huang-ti as a ruthless enemy of the people he united. The emperor's image

began to change for the better in 1958 after Chairman Mao Zedong told the Central Committee of China's Communist Party that Shih Huang-ti was more to be admired than censured because he had been the first to see the value of exterminating intellectuals who "used the past to criticize the present." Several years later, after a would-be assassin denounced the Chairman as "a contemporary Shih Huang-ti," the party apparatus went to work to prove that such a remark was actually high praise. The first emperor became the subject of laudatory articles and the party faithful were encouraged to discuss his accomplishments among themselves. Several books were also written to correct the record, the most popular of which was an official biography of Shih Huang-ti, published in 1972, that sold more than two million copies in a single year.

planted over the site to further confuse potential grave robbers, but in our time, its location near the city of Xian has become one of the most popular tourist attractions in all of China. The imperial tomb has yet to be opened, although preliminary excavations hint that its interior may still be intact. In 1974 farmers digging a well opened a hole in a nearby underground hall that contained thousands of life-size terra-cotta figures of warriors standing in formation. Two years later similar vaults were discovered yielding figures of horsemen and bronze chariots, bringing the total strength of the emperor's phantom army to more than eight thousand.

When Shih Huang-ti's tomb is finally opened, it will provide a link in the evolution of an ancient civilization that still exists. The Han Dynasty, which stayed in power for more than four hundred years (until A.D. 221), was built on the basic governmental and cultural ideas of the first emperor, and although modern China takes its name from the Chin Dynasty, its people still call themselves the Han. But the kings who created the Chinese empire obviously didn't start from scratch.

There is proof that primitive humans lived in China in the Stone Age, but there is no evidence that the ancient Chinese began using tools, building houses, or cultivating crops before 4000 B.C. Over time they began domesticating animals and gathering in communities that later organized under a single chieftan, whom legends call the Yellow Emperor, around 2000 B.C. From that moment, the Chinese seemed bent on making up for lost time and began using metal tools and weapons. Over the next few hundred years they learned to build dams and irrigation canals, discovered how to weave fabric from silk, and began to use wheels for both transportation and pottery making. They also developed a written language.

Although faraway cultures were doing the same things, there are no clues that they had any contact with the Chinese. For now at least the assumption is that the ancient Chinese developed skills on their own. Those skills flowered during the Shang Dynasty (which began in northern China in about 1600 B.C.), when the workmanship and creativity in the decorative arts far surpassed those of contemporary Near Eastern civilizations. The Shang Chinese relied on slaves captured from less sophisticated neighboring tribes to build great palaces for their kings, to fortify their cities with earthen walls as much as fifty feet (15m) thick, and to man the army. In about 1200 B.C., roughly the same time that the Near Eastern civilizations were overrun by invaders from the north, the Shang Dynasty came to an end when these slave soldiers defected to the invading Chou tribe.

The Chou ruled for the next nine centuries, during which time a new class of philosophers rose to importance. In the fifth century B.C., one of these philosophers completely changed Chinese civilization with ideas that are still at the heart of it. He spent most of his life wandering from state to state looking for a king who would make his rules of life official, but never found one. He led a small army of followers, as many as three thousand of them, who called him Kung-Kung Fu Tzu, the honorary title of "master," which has come down through the ages as "Confucius."

THE GREAT PHILOSOPHER CONFUCIUS, BORN IN 551 B.C., SPENT HIS LIFE CREATING A CODE OF HUMAN RELATIONSHIPS THAT STILL PERVADES CHINESE LIFE TODAY. ONCE ASKED FOR HIS VIEW ON LIFE AFTER DEATH, HE SAID THAT HE HAD NOT SOLVED THE MYSTERIES OF THIS LIFE AND THUS COULD NOT BE CONCERNED WITH THE NEXT.

Long before his time, Chinese culture had revolved around the concepts that the king was the Son of Heaven and that one's ancestors guided one's destiny; while Confucius confirmed these beliefs, his ideas focused more on the ways in which people lived together. He taught that everyone has an obligation to their fellow humans, but admitted that some humans are superior to others. He established rules of behavior between different classes. He also gave new structure to the family, with the oldest male as the absolute head and a hierarchy descending according to age. The family's relationship to the ruler followed the same line, with the king as the ultimate father, whose own responsibility was to heaven itself.

In the years that followed, other philosophers developed new, but usually similar, ideas in an era Chinese historians call the "Hundred Schools of Thought." Eventually, the Chinese began to regard their ideas as the basis of the world's only civilization and although they exported it in every direction, they generally considered anyone beyond the pale of their own culture as uncivilized and unworthy of any serious attention.

THE INDUS RIVER VALLEY

Historians still don't agree whether China invented its own culture or whether it owes a debt to other cultures it later considered inferior. There was an-

KING GUDEA, WHO RULED AT LAGASH IN ABOUT 2200 B.C., CREATED A RENAISSANCE IN THE ANCIENT LAND OF SUMER BY RESTORING THE OLD TEMPLES AND SHRINES AND BRINGING NEW PRIDE TO HIS PEOPLE. DURING HIS TWENTY-YEAR REIGN, HE RESTORED THE KINGDOM TO ITS ORIGINAL SIZE WITH PEACEFUL STATESMANSHIP. THIS STATUE OF GUDEA, WHICH IS IN THE LOUVRE, IS A VERY CONVINCING FORGERY.

other important civilization in the valley of the Indus River to their west that may have an older history. This civilization was well known to its neighbors, especially the earliest cultures in the Near East. The written records of this civilization in the Indus River Valley refer to cloth made from wool that grows on trees and there is evidence that the Sumerians learned about cotton from them. Early archaeologists found almost as many traces of ancient Indus cultures in Egypt and Mesopotamia as in India itself, but that changed after the British added the Indian subcontinent to their empire and began introducing modern conveniences such as the railroad.

In the 1850s the British extended their railway system through the Punjab, and workers found hundreds of thousands of old bricks that were perfect for building the roadbed. One of the British generals in charge of the project was also impressed by some clay seals with odd markings on them that he found among the bricks. It wasn't until 1921 that archaeologists went back for what the English call "a proper dig" to see what else the brick-strewn landscape might yield. What they found were the remains of a city called Harappa that had thrived for about five hundred years beginning in 2300 B.C. It was surrounded by a wall forty feet (12m) thick that extended some three and a half miles (5.5km) around. Unfortunately, most of the bricks that had been used in the buildings were now buried under the railroad, and the city's reconstruction was out of the question.

A year later another city, Mohenjo-Daro, was discovered four hundred miles (640km) away. It was nearly identical: the bricks in its buildings were exactly the same size and shape, and its streets followed a grid pattern similar to the one still favored by modern urban planners. It was a city of distinct neighborhoods broken into square blocks, some of which were lined with houses two and three stories high. Most houses, even in the poorer parts of town, had covered brick drainage systems; the streets also had drains to carry off rainwater, complete with manholes to give cleaning workers access to them. Both cities had huge granaries, whose

thick walls were laced with ventilating ducts to allow air to circulate, and workers' quarters, which some historians regard as the ancient equivalent of slums. Even the latter, however, contained drainage systems and were more solidly built than many houses in nearby modern cities.

According to the archaeologists who found these cities and have since unearthed more than sixty others, all of this indicates that the early Indus civilization was relatively wealthy as well as sophisticated. It was big, too, covering an incredible 840,000 square miles (2.2 million sq km) from present-day Delhi to Bombay, about four times as much territory as the Sumerians controlled and double the size of contemporary Egyptian kingdoms. Thousands of beautiful square seals have been found in the ancient Indus cities that contain examples of a form of writing; although more than four hundred different symbols have been isolated, no one has been able to decipher them. Possibly the greatest legacy of what is now known as the Harappan civilization was the creation of cotton fabric. The Harappans may also have been the first to domesticate the water buffalo, and there is evidence that they tamed elephants to help them with their heavy work. They were also the first culture to raise chickens for food, an important though perhaps mundane contribution to civilization.

The Harappan civilization seems to have begun to decline in the seventeenth century B.C., although no one knows for sure what happened to it. Modern historians believe that earthquakes and floods devastated its cities and changed the course of the Indus River, forcing the people to flee for their lives. The same theory also may explain why the Indo-European nomads who had been living in what is now southern Russia began wandering away from their homeland at about the same time. Many of these nomads went west and brought about the cataclysmic changes that affected most of the Near Eastern civilizations after 1200 B.C., and some of them migrated to the east into what is now Iran. One of the tribes, who called themselves "Aryans," moved still further east. And at the same time their cousins were wreaking havoc among the Sumerians

and the Egyptians, the Aryans crossed the mountains into the Indus valley.

Even though they stormed and overran cities made of brick during the first few hundred years they were in the Indus Valley, the Aryans lived (as had their ancestors in the lands they left behind) in the countryside in wooden huts. Although nothing remains of their houses, it's a good bet that none of them had indoor plumbing. Even though they found beautiful statues and figurines and intricately decorated pottery, they don't seem to have made any effort to imitate them. In spite of all that, the Aryans considered themselves the pinnacle of civilization, superior in every way to the dark-skinned people they conquered. In fact, "dasa," the word they used to describe the darker race they pushed aside, also meant "slave," and their word for themselves, "Aryan," was variously used to mean "noble." They described themselves as "wheat colored," which, to them at least, was a much more important sign of high culture than a room full of bronze statues. (Their own use of bronze was apparently limited to huge battle axes, which made them formidable warriors, as did another of their inventions, the longbow.) The Aryans had also learned to harness horses to war chariots, an innovation that had eluded the Harappans, even though the latter seem to have had a great aptitude for domesticating animals.

If the Harappan civilization is lost in the mists of time, the Aryans left behind a fairly complete record of themselves in books known as Vedas that put ancient oral traditions in writing, an art the wheat-colored people learned in about 600 B.C. One of the most important of them, the *Rig Veda*, contains more than a thousand poems describing a religious outlook that still affects life in India today. The Vedas tell us that the Aryans gradually came closer to what the modern world considers civilization, although they aren't too generous in giving any credit to the peoples they conquered. They loved music and dancing, for instance, and the excavations of Mohenjo-Daro have produced several exquisite sculptures of dancers, which might mean that the Harappans were the ones who put a song in the heart of their conquerors. The digs also produced hundreds of carved nuts that were used by the Harappans in games of dice; the later Aryans were well-known to be addicted to gambling. One Aryan legend tells of a royal family that lost its entire kingdom in a dice game, and the *Rig Veda* comments that the little numbered cubes "Cast on the board like magic bits of charcoal, though cold themselves, they burn the heart to ashes." The question of whether the Aryans appropriated the virtues and vices of existing civilizations or created their own may never be settled, but there is plenty of evidence that they were greatly influenced by the Persians in Iran who were, after all, their cultural brothers.

PERSIA

The Aryan tribes that crossed over into the Indus valley left behind two tribes of their relatives on the Iranian plateau who eventually became known as the Medes and the Persians. Like the Vedic people, they seemed content at first to go on living as simply as their ancestors had, but the civilized people already there, the Assyrians, had developed a marvelously well-organized army that frequently harassed the newcomers, especially once it was discovered that the Medes and Persians had brought beautiful horses with them. Every foray turned out to be another nail in the coffin of the Assyrian civilization because the newcomers were learning the art of war by the Assyrian example.

By 615 B.C., King Cyaxares of Media had built a copy of the Assyrian army and went off on a foray of his own. Within three years he had forged a union with the king of Babylon and after leveling the city of Nineveh began building the Achaemenidic Empire, the biggest empire the world had ever seen. It was the first to let the states it absorbed keep their own customs and elect their own local officials. It also may be the only empire in the history of the world that didn't force the conquered peoples to learn the language of the conquerors. The official tongue was Aramaic simply because it was understood by more people.

In about 550 B.C., the Median king was overthrown by a young Persian (who later became known as Cyrus the Great), and the empire became a Persian enterprise. Not much changed because Cyrus observed the Median tradition of allowing conquered people to keep their own cultural identity. But the change was noticed in Lydia, whose king, Croesus, took it as a sign that the time had come to add some territory to his own kingdom. According to Greek histories, he sent to the Oracle at Delphi for advice on how to proceed and was informed that if he attacked he would destroy a great empire. The Oracle had given a typically enigmatic message, as it later turned out. When the Lydian army was routed by the Median army, Croesus retired to his homeland for the winter, as was customary.

Croesus alerted the Egyptians, the Babylonians, and the Spartans that come spring they would all march together and destroy this upstart named Cyrus. Cyrus wasn't in a mood to wait for spring. As the Lydian army was beginning to disband for the season, the Persians marched up to the gates of Sardis, the capital of Lydia. The defenders were ready for them, but Cyrus had a secret weapon. Instead of riding to the attack on horseback, his soldiers were mounted on camels, the sight and aroma of which spooked the more traditional mounts of the Lydian cavalry; the defending army was driven back into the city.

This hardly counted as a victory, though: Sardis was widely regarded as the most impregnable city in the world at the time because of its location at the top of a steep hill. Even Cyrus thought he had been beaten. Then, after more than two weeks of siege, an odd accident gave him the key to the city. Watching a point near where the hill was steepest and least protected (because it was considered unclimbable), one of the Persian soldiers was surprised to notice a sentry on the wall lose his helmet over the side and, rather than go to the quartermaster for a new one, scramble down the hill to retrieve it. This revealed the presence of a narrow, hidden path. Following this route the next morning, the Persians entered the city in single file, killed Croesus, and claimed his legendary treasure. The "great empire" the Oracle had referred to had been Croesus' own.

When the time for war came again the following spring, the Persian armies were on the march against the Ionian cities on the west coast of Asia Minor. Cyrus was also shoring up the alliances in the east that he had inherited from the Medes. In less than ten years he more than doubled the size of his empire. He then returned to conquer Babylon, the greatest commercial city of the age, whose territory included Phoenicia, which gave him command of the sea. After Cyrus died, his son went on to conquer Egypt. The Persian expansion into India didn't take place until the emperor Darius moved the empire's eastern border to the Indus River after 521 B.C. With that, the cultures of East and West were bound together under the king of a civilization that only a century earlier was made up of nomadic farmers and herders with no concept of loyalty to any single person outside their own tribal group.

Because of the unprecedented size of their empire, the Achaemenid kings were forced to move around a lot and legend has it that they maintained five different capitals. Both Cyrus and his son preferred Babylon over the others, and excavations made in the early 1900s help to explain why. Its outer wall, ten miles (16km) around, was wide enough to allow two four-horse chariots to pass one another on the road atop the wall without slowing down. Between it and an inner wall was an ancient equivalent of the suburb, a collection of single-family houses surrounded by trees. The city itself was a magnificent collection of large buildings climaxed by a thirteen-acre (5.3ha) palace complex surrounding a garden courtyard. Twentieth-century archaeologists also uncovered what was known as the "Gate of Ishtar," a thirty-six-foot (11m) brick structure against the outer wall that was lavishly decorated with reliefs of bulls and dragons. It was the entrance to a broad triumphal highway, paved with slabs of colored stone and guarded on either side by massive stone lions. Inside, the road led across a moat and through a second inner wall to the imperial palace, inside which was the massive throne room. The king, in spite of his jewels and

golden robes, was overshadowed by the elegance of the colorful, glazed-brick walls and the statuary and carvings that surrounded him.

Every archaeologist knows that today's finds might be surpassed tomorrow. For instance, less than fifteen years after the ancient city of Babylon began revealing its secrets, an expedition from the University of Chicago's Oriental Institute found the remains of the stone palace built around 520 B.C. by Darius at Persepolis on the plain of Iran. During two years of digging, they uncovered the royal harem and defined the outline of the palace itself. In the third year they discovered what must have been an audience hall a dozen feet (3.6m) above the other rooms and, leading to it, a well-preserved stairway with a frieze six feet (1.8m) high and a thousand feet

WHEN NEBUCHADNEZZAR BECAME BABYLON'S KING IN 605 B.C., HE ORDERED A MASSIVE RESTORATION, INCLUDING A GREAT GATE TO HONOR THE GODDESS ISHTAR. THE GATE, MADE OF GLAZED BRICK, IS ADORNED WITH 575 RELIEFS OF LIONS, DRAGONS, AND BULLS. IT IS NOW IN BERLIN'S MUSEUM OF NEAR EASTERN ART.

(300m) long representing a festival attended by all the king's court and representatives of most of the states of the empire. The team, which was led by archaeologists from the University of Berlin, kept up their digging for more than eight years and found thousands of clay tablets filled with day-to-day records, jewelry and tools, and a complicated drainage system that was similar to the ones discovered at Harappa in India ten years earlier.

In the years since, the Iranian government has continued with the excavation and restoration of Persepolis and it has been discovered that the complex included three palaces. It was built on a terrace 1,500 by 900 feet (350 by 270m), cut from the solid rock of a mountainside with picks and shovels. Limestone blocks, weighing ten tons (9t) or more were hauled into place and anchored with iron bars set in molten lead. To reach the city, which was about forty feet (12.2m) above the plain, they constructed two sets of stairways that arched up the hillside, coming together on the terrace itself. The buildings were lavishly decorated with reliefs and patterns of multicolored glazed bricks and tiles. The portions of buildings made from wood were covered with plaster and painted in bright colors. In addition to a drainage system, Darius also ordered the construction of cisterns to catch and hold fresh water. Although his intention in building the city was to impress his subjects, Darius himself was apparently impressed most by the water. It was said that he wouldn't drink water from any other part of his empire and that whenever he traveled, an important part of his entourage consisted of waterbearers from Persepolis whose purpose in life was to cater to the royal thirst.

No matter how grand, how big, or how powerful an empire becomes, its days are always numbered; in the case of the Achaemenids, time began to run out after the death of the great king Xerxes, in 465 B.C. He was murdered by his son-in-law with the help of the commander of his palace guard and his chief eunuch. Xerxes had been driven out of Greece and, faced with a contracting empire, had spent his last days remodeling the string of imperial palaces in hopes that his subjects would be as impressed by his monuments as they had been by the armies of his predecessors. But his subjects interpreted the lavishness of his court as decadence and began grumbling about having to pay such high taxes to support it all. The Persians themselves paid no taxes, and that only made matters worse.

The empire did last another 130 years, however, thanks in part to the taxes it collected; it was rich enough to bribe any ruler who threatened war. Eventually, even their gold couldn't save them because Alexander, the twenty-year-old king of Macedonia, wanted something money couldn't buy: power. He had inherited one of the best armies in the world from his famous father, Philip, and in 333 B.C., Alexander took on the legendary Persian army. The last of the Persian kings, Darius III, escaped with his life, and Alexander dined that night in his tent, claiming the western half of the Persian Empire as his own. He didn't pursue Darius; instead he went on to sack the city of Tyre, then took Egypt without a struggle.

Two years later Alexander again turned his attention to the Persians. Darius was ready for him with diabolical weapons that included chariots with iron spikes to stop charging horses and sharp blades attached to their wheels; Darius even tried using elephants to stomp charging infantry to death. But Alexander's Macedonians had seen it all before and once again defeated the Persians. Darius again succeeded in escaping with his life. Even though the king still lived, Alexander marched on to Babylon, which he took without a fight, and then took the equally important Persian city of Susa, where he found the Persian royal treasury. In 330 B.C., he took possession of Persepolis, the symbol of Persian magnificence, and proceeded to burn it to the ground in demonstration of his own power. Before long, as he marched eastward toward India, Alexander found the body of King Darius, who had been murdered by his own soldiers, men whom he had deserted twice. The conqueror campaigned for seven years after that, extending his influence to the Indus valley and beyond, finally linking East and West before dying, probably from exhaustion, at the age of thirty-three.

DARIUS I IS BURIED AT NAGSH-I RUSTAM, NEAR HIS PALACE AT PERSEPOLIS, IN A TOMB (OPPOSITE PAGE) CARVED FROM THE MOUNTAIN IN THE SHAPE OF A GREEK CROSS. THE CENTRAL PORTION REPRESENTS A PALACE FACADE AND THE TOP FORMS A DAIS SUPPORTED BY THIRTY FIGURES REPRESENTING DIFFERENT PARTS OF THE PERSIAN EMPIRE.

Chapter 4

Lands of Mystery

Civilization in Africa

There is growing evidence that humans first walked upright in Africa, and in modern times, it has become more and more apparent that the continent was also the birthplace of some of the world's earliest civilizations. A climate that has destroyed many ancient artifacts and a lack of written records have added an air of mystery to ancient Africa's rich history. Some clues remain, however, and the mysteries are slowly being solved.

ZIMBABWE

In 1979, when the people of the former British colony of Southern Rhodesia became an independent nation, their constitution erased the country's colonial name and reinstated its ancient one: Zimbabwe. More accurately, the old name is Great Zimbabwe. Apart from its name, however, little is known of the stone-walled city-state that was built in southern Africa about 1,500 years ago.

When Western cultures first became aware of Zimbabwe's existence in the 1870s, there seemed to be only one possible explanation of how such an ancient fortress came to be built in a region where old civilizations, if they had existed at all, didn't leave any traces of themselves behind. A German scientist claimed that these were obviously the remains of a copy of King Solomon's Temple built by Phoenicians in the service of the Queen of Sheba. It was obvious to him anyway. As was common in Europe in those days, few people seriously believed that anyone would ever find the remnants of a civilization that wasn't mentioned in the Bible—or at least influenced by a biblical civilization. In this case, the Scriptures had provided an easy answer. The conclusion was that after the Queen of Sheba visited King Solomon she had copies of his palace built in various places, and this one in Africa was actually a warehouse for storing treasure destined for the great king. The Book of Job said that the Queen had somewhere stockpiled gold, silver, and precious gems from a far-off land called Ophir, and it seemed likely that Great Zimbabwe was the place. It was another, secular book, however, that started the rush to explore the possibility.

After H. Rider Haggard's novel *King Solomon's Mines* appeared, more than 100,000 prospectors rushed to Africa to claim their share of whatever treasure might have been left behind. Many of them managed to find what they were looking for in

abandoned mineshafts, but many more took their picks and hammers into the ruins themselves and walked off with any artifacts that seemed to be glittering, setting serious archaeology back a generation. Fortunately, the government outlawed prospecting there in 1902 and three years later researchers began sifting through the rubble.

The researchers discovered that the stone city probably wasn't built until the fourth century A.D., a long time after the days of King Solomon. The current theory is that it was designed and built by Africans without any foreign influence. The theory is still hotly debated, but it is not as controversial as the discussion of the reasons why Great Zimbabwe was built or why it was imitated in thousands of similar stone enclosures spread out over more than 270,000 square miles (700,000 sq km) south of the Zambezi River. Speculation ranges from the idea that the walls were built to keep wild animals out to the proposition that the ruins were once a kind of prison meant to keep slaves from running away.

If the actual reason for building Great Zimbabwe is ever discovered, it will probably be a fascinating one, because such an undertaking was a very un-African thing to do. The continent where many people feel human life actually began has remarkably few clues to lost civilizations, not because such communities never existed, but because most of them didn't build in stone. In most parts of Africa the soil is thin and the weather is hot and dry, making agriculture, the major impetus for city-building, a tricky business. The result was that most early Africans, at least below the Sahara, were nomads who rarely built settlements that lasted more than a growing season or two. As the Bantu peoples began migrating south, even their comparatively permanent villages were usually abandoned every decade or so. But Great Zimbabwe is an exception, and an extraordinary one at that.

The city was dominated by a hilltop fort, while the actual settlement was oddly placed on the opposite side of the fort's entrance in a valley some distance away. The settlement included an elliptical, templelike enclosure surrounded by its own wall, situated so that everything that went on behind the

© Jason Lauré

wall was visible from the fortress above. In addition to being able to make long-distance eye contact, anyone in the fortress could communicate with the valley below through an ingenious public address system. A cave under the hill with perfect natural acoustics amplified even normal conversation so that it could be heard in the valley; the sound was directed toward the Great Enclosure with a strategically placed curved wall.

Sight and sound were all that bound the hill fortress to the village below. There is no evidence of any road connecting the two or any gate that would

make it convenient to get from one to the other in time of trouble. In fact, it appears that the city planners deliberately made the fortress off-limits to the people in the valley, a different pattern from any fortified city elsewhere in the ancient world. There is also no trace anywhere near Great Zimbabwe of how they disposed of their dead, leaving archaeologists without the kinds of clues to people's lives that burial places usually provide.

In spite of the differences in the layout of the city, the hill fortress itself follows the same general plan of every other fort ever built. Its gate, however, which

THE GREAT ENCLOSURE OF ZIMBABWE IS MORE THAN EIGHT HUNDRED FEET (244M) LONG AND THIRTY-TWO FEET TALL. IT IS ONE OF THREE COMPLEXES IN THE AREA AND IS ABOUT A QUARTER-MILE (0.4 KM) AWAY FROM THE SO-CALLED ACROPOLIS, WHICH IS SITUATED HIGH ABOVE A VALLEY FILLED WITH MORE SCATTERED RUINS.

faces southeast toward the sea 250 miles (400 km) away, is almost a monument to paranoia. After winding up over a steep mountain, the road is walled on both sides, forcing a visitor, or a potential invader, to negotiate a series of sharp turns before the walls close in to create a path less than two feet (0.6 m) wide. When the path opens up again, after twisting past several guard posts, it is a corridor inside the fortress walls. The main enclosure inside the fortress covered about a quarter acre (1,000 sq m) and was surrounded by walls twenty-five feet (7.6 m) high,

which were accented by conical stone turrets. The audience rooms and living quarters beyond yielded dozens of birds carved from soapstone that not only have become the symbol of the modern country, but have yielded clues to the artistic achievements of the early Zimbabweans. Apart from the artistry of the walls themselves, there are virtually no other relics or artifacts to provide clues to the accomplishments of their ancient civilization.

Where the fortress follows traditional patterns, however, the valley ruins have a personality all their own. Among their oddities is an outer wall that could not have been more than two or three feet (0.6 or 0.9m) high, but included a gate surrounded by a high tower that enclosed a complicated path forcing anyone passing through to confront a guard. Of all the ruins, possibly the most fascinating of any that exist in Africa is the Great Enclosure itself. Among its mysteries is a tower that was once thirty-five feet (10.6m) high and almost sixty feet (18.3m) around; it is solid inside, has nothing underneath it, and shows no evidence of its top being either useful or accessible. It is the largest of five such towers inside the enclosure, not one of which has revealed the secret of its purpose. The wall that surrounds it varies from sixteen feet (4.9m) to thirty-five feet (10.6m) high and measures more than eight hundred feet (240m) around. Like every other wall in the complex, and in the other ruins in southern Africa, the stones are held together without mortar, and all of them have been cut down to small, uniform sizes that give the walls a smooth face. All of the other cultures that built in stone without bonding deliberately cut their stones large so they would hold together by their own weight, but the builders of Zimbabwe went the other way.

They broke other rules, too. Their walls were built on the ground without foundations and the builders seem to have gone around natural obstacles rather than removing them to conform to a human plan. Some theories say that they had never learned the rules of geometry and were incapable of building a straight wall with angled corners. Whatever the reason, there isn't a straight wall, either interior or exterior, anywhere in Great Zimbabwe. The walls curve in an almost sensual way and if architectural historians regard the Zimbabweans as unsophisticated, they usually admit that they were capable of creating structures of tremendous beauty.

The greatest mystery remains: who built the fortress and why? Centuries ago, a Portuguese historian wrote of an African city built of stone without mortar and claimed that Moorish merchants had reported finding an inscription over one of its doors. But he reported that "learned men who went there

DRESSED FOR SUCCESS

When Karl Mauch arrived in southern Africa from Germany in 1865, his mission was to map the landscape and test the soils for the benefit of future generations. He also, much to his annoyance, discovered gold in remote Bechuanaland, which forced him to make a decision whether to become a prosperous miner or to continue his explorations. He chose the latter and pressed on into the interior where he had been told of the existence of an ancient city that might be located in the biblical land of Ophir. Finding it, he said, was "…the highest duty in my profession to add honor to the name of the German nation." Mauch had already spent more than four years wandering through hostile unexplored territory and he knew that even if his search was successful he might not live to tell the tale. But he was willing to make a few sacrifices, the most important of which was abandoning the demands of fashion. "I had to consider it far more practical to travel with one suit only," he wrote, "probably for several years." The suit he chose was made of leather, even though he knew he would be walking under the hot African sun. He also wore a leather cap and heavy boots studded with nails and underneath it all, thick flannel underwear. "By and by one gets used it," he said. Although the outfit may have seemed better suited to an Arctic explorer than one headed for the tropics, Mauch carefully made it loose-fitting so that it trapped a layer of air inside to keep him cool in the noonday sun and comfortable in the chill of the night. He chose smooth leather, not only because it was more durable, but as he put it, because it was less likely to tear "if a naughty buffalo should suddenly force the wanderer to seek safety in flight through dangerous thorn bushes." He was traveling alone, and had to carry all his own survival gear, which included an umbrella and a wool blanket, two compasses, a barometer and a thermometer, a magnifying glass, and a pocket watch. He also carried a gun "that must be able to kill an elephant as well as a rabbit," modified to fire glass beads when his bullets ran out. His deep pockets held a pistol and a long knife as well as a hammer in case he found any interesting rocks.

The most interesting rocks Karl Mauch found were the ruins of Great Zimbabwe, which he reached in September 1871, after having spent nine months as the "white captive" of a local chief. When he finally explored the ruins, it was during what he told his captors was a routine hunting expedition, although he was careful not to tell them what he was hunting for. Subsequent excursions, carefully spaced out over a six-month period, were all under the watchful eyes of the native warriors, but Mauch was able to make sketches and maps from the concealment of the tall grass. Eventually, the white explorer was freed and allowed to return to his own world. He never went back to the Zimbabwe site, although he dreamed of making further explorations. As Mauch explained, "the next work there would consist of clearing the ruins in order to make archaeological discoveries," a step he was sure would cause ill-feeling and could be quite dangerous. The clearing and exploration of the ruins didn't begin until nearly twenty years later, after Cecil Rhodes "pacified" the area to make it safe for the business of his British South Africa Company.

did not know how to read it, nor could they tell what lettering it was in." No such writing has been discovered in modern times, but it is possible that the Zimbabweans left behind a written record of themselves and that it is waiting somewhere under those walls for someone to decipher and finally solve the riddle of Great Zimbabwe.

NORTHERN AFRICA

Oral traditions provide the only clues to most of the other civilizations of the African interior, although written records left behind by Arab traders and others often confirm those clues. One day the earth will probably give up traces of such empires as Ghana in the western Sudan. For almost nine hundred years, beginning in A.D. 200, the Ghanians provided gold, ivory, and slaves for the outside world and grew fabulously rich in the process. It was said that their king lived in a palace whose balconies were made of pure gold and had a stable big enough for a thousand horses. His capital city, probably located in present-day Mauretania, fell to Moslem invaders in the twelfth century and vanished from the face of the earth. It was replaced with another African empire, Mali, whose king, in the words of an Egyptian historian, was "the most powerful, the richest, the most fortunate" of all the African rulers who ever lived. His capital city, Timbuktu, was

burned to the ground by Mossi warriors in the fifteenth century and yet another civilization was lost. "Lost," however, is a relative term. In today's world, the legacies of Ghana and Mali and dozens of other African cultures are only waiting to be rediscovered.

The earliest settlers in the Nile Valley came from the mountain regions to the south. The history of Egypt is filled with contributions to its civilization from its African neighbors, especially the Nubians, who provided the kingdom with soldiers and most of its gold, not to mention, as historians are now saying, some of its pharaohs. When Egypt began to go into decline in the first millenium B.C., its traditions and its glory moved southward into the African empire of Kush, below the Nile's Fourth Cataract.

The history of Kush is entwined with that of Egypt, but Kush broke away from Egyptian control in 950 B.C. Two hundred years later, Kush annexed the Upper Kingdom, taking control of all the territory from the Sahara to Ethiopia and from the Mediterranean south to Khartoum. Even after the Assyrians conquered Egypt three hundred years later, the rulers of Kush kept the old Egyptian civilization alive for another thousand years. Their capital at Meroe still holds most of its secrets, but the little that has been excavated so far points to a rich culture that added touches of its own to ideas imported from Egypt. Its pottery is often called the finest produced by any ancient people, and there is evidence of influence from (or on) India in extensive carvings of lions and elephants.

The empire finally collapsed after Egypt became part of the Roman Empire, and although the Kushites left traces of their glories, there is no clue as to what became of them in the end. Their language has never been deciphered and their cities haven't been completely explored. The last record of the Kushites, left behind when the Romans pulled out of Africa in A.D. 350, says that their towns were burned and their temples pulled down. No one knows what became of their priests and rulers or the people who created their art. It is generally believed they wandered west into the heart of Africa, but no trace of them has ever been found.

THE MONOLITHIC CHURCH OF ST. GEORGE AT ETHIOPIA'S HOLY CITY OF LALIBELA WAS CARVED IN THE SHAPE OF A CROSS FROM A SINGLE BLOCK OF ROCK. ITS THIRTEENTH-CENTURY BUILDERS FIRST ISOLATED THE BLOCK BY EXCAVATING THE STONE AROUND IT, THEN CARVED IT INSIDE AND OUT TO CREATE THE CHURCH.

© Haroldo and Flavia de Faria Castro/FPG International

The origins of the Kushites are lost in the myths and legends of antiquity, too. Their name seems to come from the biblical account of Noah's curse of slavery on the sons of Ham, one of whom was named Kush. Early Greek translations of the Bible point to a deeper connection between the people and the region by referring to the Kushites as "Aethiops," meaning "burnt faces." Ethiopian historians, grasping at that crumb and enhancing it with the tale that their country was founded by the Queen of Sheba, claimed that theirs was the oldest civilized country in the world. This is not true, of course, but it is, except for Rome, the world's oldest Christian country; in fact, most of the traces of its civilization are related to Christianity, which gained a foothold there in A.D. 333.

The most impressive Christian monuments in the region are hundreds of twelfth-century churches, many of which were carved from solid rock, including the Church of the Redeemer of the World, which is one hundred feet (30m) long, seventy feet (21m) wide, and thirty-six feet (11m) high, hollowed out from a giant red boulder. Although the idea of carving monuments from existing rock was popular among the Egyptians, many historians suggest that the Ethiopian church builders weren't imitating their ancient neighbors to the west, but that the people of the Nile had learned such things from the ancestors of the Ethiopians, the Abyssinians. We may never know for sure.

The ancient Ethiopians didn't leave many traces of themselves, but the ruins of their capital at Aksum have yielded several impressive upright stone slabs known as stelae, including one that, although now broken into pieces, once rose an impressive one hundred and ten feet (33m) high, the largest ever found anywhere. Another, only sixty-five feet (20m) high, was so beautifully carved that when the Italians invaded Ethiopia in the 1930s, Mussolini had it shipped back to Rome. Considering the number of stelae and other remnants of old civilizations already in Rome, taking the African monument was a form of high praise for the lost civilization of Aksum. Of course, the Ethiopians didn't quite see it that way and they are still trying to get it back.

THE HUGE OBELISKS AT AKSUM IN PRESENT-DAY ETHIOPIA WERE CARVED IN ABOUT 500 B.C. FROM SINGLE BLOCKS OF STONE. THEY RESEMBLE SKYSCRAPERS WITH ORDERLY ROWS OF WINDOWS, BUT THERE ARE NO DECIPHERABLE INSCRIPTIONS TO SOLVE THE MYSTERY OF THEIR ORIGINAL FUNCTION.

East of Eden

The Americas before Columbus

On his third voyage to the New World, Christopher Columbus discovered the mouth of the Orinoco river and began to think for the first time that he hadn't reached Asia, but had found what he called "the earthly paradise whither no one can go save by God's permission." He had found Eden itself.

MÉRIDA, THE CAPITAL CITY OF THE MEXICAN STATE OF YUCATÁN, WAS THE MAYAN TOWN OF TIHÓ UNTIL THE SPANISH TOOK IT OVER IN 1542. THE CONQUERORS, WHO THOUGHT THE STONEWORK OF THE MAYANS RESEMBLED BUILDINGS THE ROMANS HAD LEFT BEHIND AT MÉRIDA, SPAIN, RENAMED THE PLACE. THIS ENORMOUS STATUE (PAGE 66) IS LOCATED AT MÉRIDA.

THE GOD OF THE SUN, WHOSE MASK (PREVIOUS PAGE) ADORNED BUILDINGS IN ALL MAYAN CITIES, WAS VERY IMPORTANT TO THESE AGRICULTURAL PEOPLE. IN ADDITION TO THIS DEITY, THE MAYAN PANTHEON INCLUDED FOUR RAIN GODS KNOWN AS CHACS, EACH OF WHICH REPRESENTED A DIFFERENT POINT OF THE COMPASS.

It was an understandable conclusion. By the fifteenth century, it was widely conceded that all the dry land in the world was distributed among three continents. The authority was the Bible itself, which speaks only of Asia, Africa, and Europe. Everyone believed that if there were any other land-masses, God would have revealed them when He caused the Scriptures to be written. But Genesis did say that there was another land east of the sunrise and that a river went out from it and parted into four heads. Three of them were identified: one, the Bible says, surrounded Ethiopia, another flowed into Assyria, and the third became the Euphrates. But the other was a puzzlement. "The name of the first is Pison," says Genesis, "that is it which compasseth the whole land of Havilah, where there is gold: And the gold of that land is good."

Columbus sincerely believed that he had found the mouth of that river and that somewhere beyond, at the point closest to heaven on the top of a high mountain, was the earthly paradise created for Adam and Eve. Others were more intrigued by the idea that there was gold there. Less than forty years later their search for it ended with the death of a highly advanced civilization; the Incan emperor Atahualpa was murdered and his people were introduced to Spanish-style civilization.

SOUTH AMERICA

The Incan empire covered most of South America's west coast, including all of what is now Peru, Ecuador, and Bolivia and large parts of Colombia and Argentina. Ancient Incan legends suggest that the first Inca and his sister were created by the Sun God on an island in Lake Titicaca in the twelfth century A.D. Archaeologists haven't found evidence that their descendants began building their empire until three hundred years later, not long before the Spanish came, but they have found traces of human life in the Andes dating back more than 10,000 years. In addition, ruins of a multistoried temple, built by a people called the Chavín, north of present-day Lima, points to a civilization that existed in the

eighth century B.C. Chavín sculpture, though still mysterious, provides hints that they grew corn and that they wove cloth; not much else is known about them. Later cultures along the coast were even more highly advanced, creating sophisticated pottery and beautifully patterned cloth. And long before the Incas arrived to conquer them, the Chavíns built great cities, including the Chimu capital, Chan-Chan, which covered eight square miles (21 sq km) and contained pyramids and irrigated gardens. Yet the Incan legends say that before they built their city in the Cuzco Valley, all the tribes they would soon conquer were uncivilized.

THE INCAN CITY OF CUZCO WAS BUILT IN THE FORM OF A PUMA, WITH ITS HEAD REPRESENTED BY THE FORTRESS OF SAQSAYWAMAN. WHEN THE SPANISH ARRIVED, ONE OF THEM WROTE OF CUZCO THAT "NEITHER THE BRIDGE OF SEGOVIA NOR ANY OF THE BUILDINGS THAT HERCULES OR THE ROMANS BUILT ARE AS WORTHY OF BEING SEEN AS THIS."

Once the Incan empire was established, it was divided into four provinces. All of its major cities followed the same master plan, with public buildings around a central square and narrow streets in a pattern that was usually dictated by the terrain. Many of them counted their population in the hundreds, but the center of the empire, Cuzco, was home to nearly a quarter million people. The two rivers that cut through it were channeled into canals and drinking water was available from troughs in the middle of the streets. The streets themselves were arranged in a grid pattern around two plazas, the larger of which was dominated by the massive

Temple of the Sun. The city was divided into districts and housed representatives from every corner of the empire. These representatives could be identified by their tribal headdress, which they were required to wear. The chiefs of subject tribes all lived in the great city, which gave it an elegance that would probably be described as "international" in a modern city, but which the Spanish conquerors described as "exotic."

Cuzco's important buildings were constructed of long stones fitted together with remarkable precision; none of the Incan architecture featured any carved decoration. Many of the more important

GRAVEN IMAGES

Most of the gold artifacts of the Aztecs and Incas were melted down into ingots to make it easier to ship across the Atlantic to the royal treasury of Spain. While the Spaniards were clearly dazzled by the riches they found, some of the missionaries among them were fascinated by the civilizations that had made the treasures. One of the missionaries, Fr. Bernadino de Sahagún, learned Nahuatl, the language of the Aztecs, and spent years interviewing them in a search for clues to their heritage. In the process, he produced twelve books on his findings, which are still considered basic to any study of the customs of the Aztecs. Another Spanish friar, Diego de Landa, was intrigued by the buildings the Mayans had left behind on the Yucatán Peninsula and wrote glowing descriptions of them. De Landa didn't seem to have had much admiration for the descendants of the Mayans, however; he was one of the few recalled to Spain to stand trial for cruelty to the Indians. Before he left, he went on a rampage, smashing sculptures and burning books, wiping out centuries of the history of a culture he claimed to admire. "They contain nothing in which there was not to be seen superstitions and lies of the devil," he said.

© Van Phillips/Leo deWys

palaces and temples were covered with gold plates, some weighing as much as ten pounds (4.5 kg), which proved to be the greatest single source of Incan gold that was eventually hauled off to Spain. What impressed the conquistadors most was a fantastic structure they called the Golden Enclosure. It consisted of six temples surrounding an open courtyard whose centerpiece was a huge fountain made of solid gold. The plaza also had a "garden" whose cornstalks were wrought from pure gold, and even the representation of the dirt under them was made of gold. There were also solid-gold sculptures of two dozen llamas and life-size statues of the shepherds who tended them. And there was more. As one of the bedazzled Spaniards wrote: "If I were to recount all the different varieties in the shape of gold, my story would never end." Of course, the story did end. All of the gold was melted down into ingots destined for the royal treasury in Madrid.

Even though Incan civilization disappeared, it left behind a perfect snapshot of itself in a place called Machu Picchu, more than eight thousand feet (2,400m) up in the high Andes. Neither Spanish nor Incan legends mention such a place, and it wasn't until 1911 that the U.S. explorer Hiram Bingham found it, just as its original inhabitants had left it. Because of its isolation, Machu Picchu represents one of the few perfectly preserved abandoned cities in the world; because many parts of it are still unexcavated, the city still holds its share of mysteries. The biggest mystery is why the Incas went to so much trouble to build a hanging city in such an inaccessible place. It is believed that it was part of a chain of such fortresses, each about twelve miles (19km) apart, that were connected to Cuzco by a stone road. Of all of them, this one must have been considered the ultimate hardship post: it is a city of terraced gardens and stairways with more than three thousand steps to help its residents get from place to place, and is the only Incan city yet found that was enclosed behind a wall. The buildings themselves are solidly built and like all Incan architecture, completely undecorated. The opposite is true of the buildings created by other, earlier civilizations to the north.

ALTHOUGH MACHU PICCHU (OPPOSITE PAGE) IS THE MOST VISITED OF THE INCAN MONUMENTS, TOUR GUIDES CAN ONLY OFFER EDUCATED GUESSES ABOUT ITS ORIGINAL FUNCTION. IT MAY HAVE BEEN A FORTIFIED FRONTIER OUTPOST, A SANCTUARY FOR MOON WORSHIPERS, OR EVEN, SOME SAY, A WORK CENTER USED EXCLUSIVELY BY WOMEN. THE ENTIRE COMPLEX OF MACHU PICCHU (ABOVE) WAS CAREFULLY PLANNED TO TAKE FULL ADVANTAGE OF THE TERRAIN. THE RESIDENTIAL SECTION IS SEPARATED FROM THE AGRICULTURAL ZONE, AND A PLAZA DIVIDED THE UPPER AND LOWER CITY. ITS TWO HUNDRED BUILDINGS PROBABLY HOUSED A POPULATION OF ABOUT ONE THOUSAND. WHEN ARCHAEOLOGISTS EXPLORED THE ROYAL PALACE AT THE INCAN TOWN OF HUÁNUCO, THEY FOUND A CACHE OF THOUSANDS OF POTS, PITCHERS, AND OTHER POTTERY (LEFT). THEY CONCLUDED THAT THE POTTERY HAD BEEN USED FOR ELABORATE *TAQUI* FEASTS THAT CELEBRATED THE HARVEST AND ENDED LONG, TRADITIONAL PERIODS OF FASTING.

MACHU PICCHU (LEFT) SITS HIGH IN THE ANDES ON A NATURAL SADDLE DOMINATED BY THE MOUNTAIN PEAK CALLED HUAYNA PICCHU. IT IS BELIEVED THAT IT WAS BUILT IN THE FIFTEENTH CENTURY AND WAS THE LAST REFUGE OF THE INCAS AFTER THE SPANISH INVASION; IT WAS ONCE THOUGHT TO HAVE BEEN THE BIRTHPLACE OF THE FIRST INCA. A STAIRWAY CUT INTO THE ROCK (ABOVE) LEADS TO THE HOUSE OF THE *ÑUSTA*, "THE PRINCESS," AND THE *TORREÓN*, WHOSE CURVING WALLS, RARE IN INCAN ARCHITECTURE, LED HIRAM BINGHAM, WHO DISCOVERED MACHU PICCHU, TO IDENTIFY IT AS THE CITY'S SUN TEMPLE.

THE OPEN PLAZA OF THE MAYAN CITY OF CHICHÉN ITZÁ IN THE YUCATÁN IS DOMINATED BY THE TEMPLE OF KUKULCAN, WHICH THE SPANISH RENAMED EL CASTILLO. IT WAS DEDICATED TO THE WORSHIP OF THE FEATHERED SERPENT GOD QUETZALCOATL.

© Grace Davies/Photo Network

CENTRAL AMERICA

Some of the most lavishly carved structures left behind by any vanished race are those of the Mayans in Central America and southern Mexico. Of all the ancient races of the Americas, they were the only ones who carved written records of themselves in stone. Virtually every inch of their buildings is covered with intricate murals and glyph writing, but most of it has yet to be deciphered. And although thousands of books have been written about the Mayans since Columbus met a party of them off the coast of Honduras in 1502, most of what is known about them amounts to educated guesses.

It is believed that the original Mayans arrived on the Mexican Gulf Coast in about 2000 B.C.; they developed a civilization that thrived for 3,500 years, until the Spanish converted them to Christianity. Over those years, they developed a sophisticated calendar, created a written language, and built hundreds of stone cities. Most evidence supports the theory that the great Mayan cities were built in the 1,500 years after 500 B.C., but there is no clue as to why these cities were later abandoned to the jungle. There is no sign of any destruction, either by natural forces or by invading armies, but for reasons that are still a mystery, the Mayans deserted the cities that had taken them centuries to build and relocated in the mountains of Guatemala and in a corner of the Yucatán.

After moving the Mayans found themselves in closer contact with the Toltecs, a classical civilization centered to the north of modern Mexico City. Beginning in the ninth century, Mayans and Toltecs lived together at Chichén Itzá in the Yucatán. Not long afterward, they built the nearby city of Uxmal and then Mayapán, which became the first capital of the Mayans, who until that time had never singled out one of their cities as more important than the others.

The Mayans changed in other ways, too. Their art began to include representations of Quetzalcoatl, the half man, half serpent who first appeared among the Toltecs, as well as other fearsome beasts such as eagles and jaguars. Their religion began to include human sacrifice and their young men began training in the arts of war. This all represented a kind of renaissance for the Mayans. Although they became more aggressive, they also began building bigger and more beautiful pyramids and temples. The city of Uxmal is still considered one of the most beautiful ever built in ancient America. Their art became more refined and their pottery more exquisite. Their place in history as the New World's first true intellectuals was assured. All this came to an end, however, in a civil war that led to an Itza attack on Mayapán in A.D. 1441, after which the capital city was abandoned forever.

What is known of the Mayans first came to light at the ruins of Palenque in modern Honduras, which was first explored by the Spanish in 1773. Next on the scene was a Viennese count who arrived in 1832 with the news that "I am the first competent person who occupied himself with the ruins of Central America." Be that as it may, eight years later the American John Lloyd Stevens arrived on the scene and began disproving the count's assertions that the city had been built by Romans, or possibly Phoenicians.

What has been uncovered in the years since is a city built over a river that was forced through an arched underground channel. Its palace, measuring 340 by 240 feet (103 by 73m), and rising up to sixty feet (18m), includes a courtyard with a four-story tower that has an interior stairway. Its outer walls are covered with relief figures carved in stucco and inside are plaques with inscriptions carved in stone. Other structures seem to be temples built in the form of pyramids. Although explorations are continuing, the ruins of Palenque are, like most of the Mayan cities, almost invisible in the thick jungle, which makes them all the more mysterious, especially early in the day, when thick fog covers them in mist.

The jungles have also swallowed up the remains of what many consider the first of the civilized peoples of the Americas, the Olmecs, who created a religion based on magic at about the same time that Neolithic hunters began settling down to grow corn. Their magic, which they said came from the jaguar

© Steven D. Elmore/Tom Stack and Associates

god, made it possible, they claimed, for them to control the rains. They also said that the fertility of the soil was guaranteed if humans were sacrificed to the gods, an idea that pervaded every culture that followed theirs.

On a less gruesome note, they also learned to process rubber from the trees that grew in the rainforests where they lived, and shaped it into balls that they used in ritual games that also long outlived them. They showed their neighbors how to weave cloth from cotton, and their skill at stone carving probably inspired many civilizations that followed theirs. Their greatest magic, however, was a calendar that allowed them to keep track of the seasons. It was indispensable to farmers and the Olmec priests took care that only they knew the secret of how to read it.

THE GREAT CLASSIC MAYAN CITY OF TEOTIHUACÁN IN THE CENTER OF MODERN MEXICO, OFTEN CALLED THE "ABODE OF THE GODS," WAS A POWERFUL POLITICAL CENTER OF MERCHANTS, WARRIORS, AND KINGS. IT REACHED ITS PEAK OF INFLUENCE IN ABOUT A.D. 200.

© Art Resource: Pyramid of the Sun, Teotihuacan

THE BUILDINGS OF TEOTIHUACÁN, INCLUDING ITS GREAT PYRAMID OF THE SUN, AFFECTED THE ARCHITECTURE OF THE ENTIRE MAYAN WORLD. THE CITIES THAT GREW IN ITS IMAGE AS FAR AWAY AS HONDURAS AND EL SALVADOR BECAME, IT IS OFTEN SAID, MORE MEXICAN THAN TRADITIONAL MAYAN.

many ways, the ancient American cultures had no domesticated work animals and no metal tools, and never discovered the wheel. The smaller but more graceful Pyramid of the Moon was surrounded by twelve temples; the nearby citadel also had twelve temples and a pyramid.

The city of Teotihuacán was built over several centuries, following a plan devised around 200 B.C. It covered about eight square miles (21 sq km) and had cement-paved streets with a system of drains to carry off rainwater. The surrounding countryside was criss-crossed with irrigation canals that watered farms over an area of more than a thousand square miles (2,600 sq km). Later civilizations remembered it as "The Place Where Men Became Gods," but nothing else is known about the men who built Teotihuacán, including what language they might have spoken. It isn't known what became of them, either. Some time between A.D. 600 and 700, they simply ceased to exist.

Their ghosts continued to influence other civilizations, and from the time they vanished nearly all the art and architecture was based on their models, with few signs of innovation. When the last of the invaders arrived from the north in the twelfth century, the Valley of Mexico was divided into a half dozen city-states, each trying to impress the others with their temples and palaces, most of which were not much different from the others. Those last invaders, the Aztecs, who called themselves the "Mexica," changed everything. They were far more warlike than the people they had moved in on, and the kings in the valley put aside their own differences, uniting to force the Aztecs to settle in a snake-infested swamp in hopes they would become disgruntled and go away.

The Aztecs thrived, however, and that prompted the kings to remove them to even more hostile mud flats, which also proved to be a mistake. The Aztecs didn't prosper there, but their predicament brought them closer together and sharpened their hate for their new neighbors. Furthermore, they had a strong religious belief to sustain them: an old prophecy related that they would one day establish an empire in a place that would be identified by an

After the Olmecs vanished in about 700 B.C., other priests figured out how to use the calendar and some improved on it. A few hundred years later, the understanding of astronomy that made the calender work made it possible for them to build Teotihuacán, the biggest city anywhere in the world at the time. Its centerpiece was the Pyramid of the Sun, built around A.D. 100, which soared more than two hundred feet (61m) from a seven-hundred-foot (213m) base. Like the pyramids of Egypt, it was built by human brawn. Although sophisticated in eagle perched on a cactus. When the bird was spotted, it was devouring a rattlesnake, an addition that was interpreted to mean that they would have to devour their neighbors before their empire would become a reality. Within a century they had devoured all the cultures in central and southern Mexico.

By the time Montezuma II became emperor of the Aztecs (ten years after Columbus sailed into the Caribbean), he ruled over a territory larger than modern Italy with a population of more than thirty million. Even France, the biggest country in Europe at the time, had a population of less than twenty million, and Spain, with only eight million, was puny by comparison. No city anywhere, not in France, not in Italy, not in Spain, was as big or as grand as Montezuma's capital of Tenochtitlán. Its population was about 250,000 at a time when none of the four biggest cities in Europe had even half that many citizens. Tenochtitlán was also one of the first cities in the history of the world to be surrounded by suburbs.

Like Venice, the Aztec capital was built on an island of reclaimed land. Although they had their choice of any spot in the Valley of Mexico, they chose to stay in the mud flats their ancestors had been banished to because it was there that the snake-eating eagle had prophesied their destiny. Over time, they had transformed the muddy bottom of Lake Texcoco into about five square miles (13 sq km) of living space by driving pilings into the marsh to support the buildings. More dry land was created when they built a seven-mile (11.2 km) dike to hold back the water of the lake, and they added the illusion of even more space by inventing floating gardens. The city was interlaced with canals, all of them bulkheaded in stone, and was connected to the mainland by three wide causeways that included sections that could be lifted to allow access by large boats. Tenochtitlán also had a public zoo and well-tended botanical gardens; the streets that ran alongside the canals were washed every day and every night garbage was hauled away in barges.

The emperor lived in a hundred-room palace where the air was scented with incense. He had a huge swimming pool overlooking the lake and three thousand servants at his beck and call. His harem was said to include a thousand women and it was said that at dinnertime he had his choice of a hundred dishes, not selected from a menu, but all prepared and ready to eat. However sophisticated Aztec civilization seems now, the Spanish conquistador Hernando Cortés seems to have believed his own was better.

When Cortés and his men arrived at Tenochtitlán, they were received as gods rather than conquerors. An old prophecy had convinced the Aztecs that the serpent god Quetzalcoatl would return to reclaim his earthly kingdom and they were sure that Cortés was no less a person than Quetzalcoatl himself. The Spaniards were given a palace of their own,

THE OLMEC, THE FIRST CULTURE IN MEXICO TO CREATE GREAT ART, MAY HAVE EMERGED AS EARLY AS 900 B.C. THEIR MOST SPECTACULAR CREATIONS WERE HUGE HEADS CARVED FROM BLOCKS OF BASALT, SOME OF WHICH ARE NINE FEET (2.7M) HIGH AND WEIGH UP TO TEN TONS (9,072 KG) EACH. THE STONE WAS QUARRIED MORE THAN EIGHTY MILES (129 KM) AWAY.

but although they liked being treated as gods, they knew they weren't and as a precaution against trickery, they took Montezuma prisoner. Claiming it was just a formality, the Spaniards said they were there to help the emperor expand his territory and began ranging through the countryside, helping themselves to any gold they found. Eventually their greed got out of hand and their Aztec hosts revolted. After a week of fighting in the streets of the city, the Spanish decided to retreat to the mainland, but couldn't resist taking all the treasure they could carry. Their burdens cost most of them their lives when they met Aztec warriors on the causeways.

Cortés and a handful of survivors managed to escape into the mountains, where they met up with more Spanish soldiers, and, after recruiting thousands of native warriors with little love for the Aztecs, they went back for revenge. The siege of Tenochtitlán lasted more than three months, even

though the invaders had complete control of the lake and the advantage of gunpowder. By the time it ended almost all of the city had been destroyed and Cortés finished the job by burning what was left. The pitifully few survivors were tortured to death and the great Aztec empire became a memory.

Their own legends say that the Aztecs originated in the deserts of the north, which is now called the American Southwest, and most ethnologists agree that the pre-Columbian civilizations were close relatives of the people usually called Native Americans. After their experiences in Peru and Mexico, the Spanish were easily convinced that there were more civilizations with more treasures farther north, and when they were told that there were seven cities in a land called Cíbola, whose streets were paved with gold and whose palaces were studded with precious stones, they felt it was their Christian duty to find those cities.

NORTH AMERICA

It turned out to be a wild goose chase, but the conquistadors did find a civilization that lived in impressive cities that one of their chroniclers said were "made of good worked stone with gates and gutters like a city in Castile." High praise, indeed, but they soon found even more sophisticated city-states whose people lived in what must have seemed like skyscrapers to sixteenth-century Europeans. The cliff-dwellings the Spanish called "pueblos" still exist in New Mexico and Arizona in places like Mesa Verde and Chaco Canyon, and there are probably hundreds of similar dwellings that still haven't been found.

Among the undiscovered is the lost city of Luka-chukai, which may or may not be in Arizona. Just after the turn of the century, a pair of explorers were surprised when their Navajo guide disappeared among the rocks and came back with a big ceramic pot of the sort that was found in many ancient pueblos. He reported that there were others where he had found the pot and that they came from a place with big houses and towers all filled with unbroken vases and pots as well as unfaded blankets. But when they asked him where this place was, he refused to answer, saying that it belonged to the Old Ones, whom the Navajo call Anasazi, and shouldn't be disturbed. With that the young Indian disappeared again, saying he must return the pot; he reappeared empty-handed and refused to tell them anything more. The white men decided to leave well enough alone. It would be simple to find their campsite again another year, they thought, and from there they would eventually find this lost city the boy told them was called Lukachukai. After several seasons of searching, they weren't even able to find their base camp. The lost city is still lost.

THE ARRIVAL OF HOSTILE TRIBES FROM THE NORTH FORCED THE INDIANS OF THE SOUTHWEST TO BUILD THEIR PUEBLOS IN CLIFFSIDE CAVES OR ON HIGH LEDGES. THEIR ADOBE HOUSES WERE AS UNASSAILABLE AS ANY MEDIEVAL CASTLE, BUT THE INDIANS WERE FORCED TO GROW THEIR FOOD ON HIGH MESAS, WHERE THEY WERE EASY PREY.

MYSTERIOUS MOUNDS, LIKE THIS ONE (BELOW, RIGHT) IN WISCONSIN, INTRIGUED AMERICANS FOR GENERATIONS. IT IS BELIEVED THAT THEY WERE THE BURIAL SITES OF PRIESTS AND CHIEFS OF ANCESTORS OF THE AMERICAN INDIANS, THE ADENA, WHO EMERGED IN ABOUT 800 B.C., AND THE HOPEWELL, WHO THRIVED SOME SIX HUNDRED YEARS LATER.

MOST OF THE ANCIENT MOUNDS IN NORTH AMERICA SEEM TO BE BURIAL SITES, AND THE ARTIFACTS THEY CONTAIN WERE PROBABLY FOR USE IN THE AFTERLIFE. IN THE SOUTHERN APPALACHIANS, HOWEVER, THESE MOUNDS MAY HAVE BEEN CREATED AS TEMPLES. THESE SCULPTURES (OPPOSITE PAGE), FOUND IN GEORGIA, INDICATE A PRACTICE OF ANCESTOR WORSHIP.

The pueblos of the Southwest are probably the best clues we have that the people who originally lived in what is now the United States created civilizations. When the English and others began establishing colonies in North America, they sought out symbols of lost civilizations in the new land. As they pushed west they thought they found them at last in the form of great mounds of earth. There were at least ten thousand of them in the Ohio River valley alone and thousands more near the Mississippi River, some as much as one hundred feet (305m) high. Most were too regular and symmetrical to be anything but man-made, and when some were attacked with spades, they were found to contain weapons and jewelry quite unlike the kind used by contemporary Indian tribes.

Over time, amateur archaeologists discovered that not all the mounds were the same. Up near the Great Lakes the mounds were usually low and often

had the shape of birds and beasts; along the Ohio River they tended to be conical; and near the lower Mississippi they were more likely to be in the form of pyramids. Their mysteries intrigued everyone, including Thomas Jefferson, who added archaeology to his long list of accomplishments in 1781 when he took a spade to a mound on his Virginia plantation. He found that it was filled with human bones, which were the remains, he estimated, of about a thousand people. What made his dig significant was that he made perpendicular cuts to reveal different states of decay in what he called the different "strata" of the mound. (With that, he established a methodology called stratigraphy that is still used by modern archaeologists without which they would find it far more difficult to determine the ages of the things they find.)

Most of the early explorations of the mysterious American mounds were not as scientific or as me-

thodical as Thomas Jefferson's. All through the nineteenth century, the mounds fascinated Americans, most of whom accepted on faith that they must have been built by visitors from civilized lands. Just about any culture that had ever made a pile of dirt, from the Israelites to the Vikings to the Romans and even the usual suspects, the Phoenicians, must have visited the Americas in ancient times, they said. The theories were finally put to rest in 1890 after the Smithsonian Institution formed America's first team of professional archaeologists, who concluded that the great mounds were built by Native Americans without any outside help. "It was an alluring conjecture that a powerful people, superior to the Indians, once occupied the Valley of the Ohio and the Appalachian ranges," said their report. As far as they were concerned, at least, the idea of a lost race in North America was a "romantic fallacy." But a lost civilization? Perhaps.

THE SECRETS OF THE MOUND BUILDERS

In 1879, when the U.S. government appropriated funds for the Smithsonian Institution to study Native American cultures, they selected John Wesley Powell, the man who had been first to explore the depths of the Grand Canyon, as the project's head. In his years as a geological explorer, Powell became fascinated by the accomplishments of the western tribes. He was furious when Congress diverted part of his budget in efforts to prove that the ancient mound builders could not have been red men, but rather a race with origins in Europe. Powell became single-minded about proving Congress wrong and hired the archaeologist Cyrus Thomas to find supporting evidence. The crash program involved probing more than two thousand mounds from Florida to North Dakota. In the process, his crews unearthed some 40,000 artifacts, which Thomas used to confirm the fact that the mounds were built by the ancestors of the people Europeans found on the American continent centuries later. The project had to be completed in a short time (by archaeological standards), not because of the competition from others with a different axe to grind, but because landowners had found a lucrative market among collectors for the artifacts buried under the mounds. These treasures were disappearing at an alarming rate. Most of the sites probed by the Smithsonian teams in the 1880s have since been destroyed, but few as thoroughly as the Spiro Mound in Oklahoma, which became famous as a source of ancient pottery in the 1930s. At first, the diggers were content to scratch the mound's surface with spades, but in the interest of efficiency they hired former miners to dig tunnels into the earthwork. As a result, pots, beads, and fabrics were removed by the carload. So many artifacts were taken that their value began to drop dramatically, which prompted the shortsighted entrepreneurs to cut off the supply by dynamiting what was left of the conical hill.

Chapter 6

Back to Nature

Angkor and Easter Island

At about the same time the great Romanesque cathedral and its leaning tower were being built at Pisa in Italy, and the Gothic masterpieces Notre Dame de Paris and the cathedral at Chartres were being built by the French, thousands of workers were putting the finishing touches on the largest

83

© Wolfgang Kaehler

THE HUGE CARVED HEADS (PAGE 82) THAT COVER THE TOWERS OF THE BAYON AT THE CENTER OF CAMBODIA'S ANGKOR THOM HAVE THEIR LIPS TURNED UPWARD AT THE EDGES IN ETERNAL SMILES. ALTHOUGH THESE HEADS SEEM TO CONVEY A REASSURING FRIENDLINESS, SOME MODERN VISITORS ARE UNNERVED BY THE GRINNING FACES.

FIGURES OF *APSARAS* (PREVIOUS PAGE), HEAVENLY DANCERS, APPEAR EVERYWHERE ON THE WALLS OF ANGKOR WAT. AN EARLY EXPLORER DESCRIBED THEM AS "EXTREMELY SENSUAL," BUT HAD TO ADD THAT HE FOUND THEM "COMPLETELY SEXLESS." IT MAY BE BECAUSE THEY ARE RELIGIOUS FIGURES, REPRESENTING WOMEN WHO WELCOME THE PIOUS TO HEAVEN.

religious building in the world, the temple of Angkor Wat. In addition, an enigmatic civilization stranded in the Pacific Ocean was in decline.

INDOCHINA

A largely abandoned ruin in the Cambodian rain-forest, Angkor Wat still has the power to command reverential silence and inspire wild flights of imagination. Anyone visiting Angkor Wat today can easily be transported back eight centuries to a time when parades of elephants draped in silk and gold marched across the stone bridge over the almost mile (1.6km) -long moat that surrounds it. The mind's eye can see lavishly dressed nobles swaying in their perches on the elephants' backs and lines of servants following them with colorful banners and bright parasols. It seems possible to hear the gongs that are beaten to keep long lines of soldiers in step, and to capture the sound of the wheels of chariots pulled by lumbering buffaloes.

The Khmer people who created Angkor Wat, and whose descendants are providing the labor to restore it, lived for long centuries as part of the great Chinese-influenced kingdom called Funan, which also included Laos, Vietnam, Thailand, and Malaysia. The great temple and more than seventy others covering some twenty-five square miles (65 sq km) in what was once the capital city of Angkor seems more a monument to the culture of India than to either the Chinese or the Khmers. They were built as Hindu temples and only much later became holy places for Buddhists. Indian influence came in the form of spice-trading merchants who gave Funan a Brahmin king in about A.D. 400; for a thousand years, the Khmer were the favored people of the new kingdom. After the Thais rebelled and destroyed their neighbors' cities in the fourteenth century, however, the jungle began to reclaim the ruins, which were virtually forgotten for hundreds of years afterwards.

In 1860 Henri Mouhot, a French naturalist hunting for rare butterflies, stumbled on the ruins, which he said suddenly transported him "as if by enchantment from barbarism to civilization, from darkness to light." Others followed him, but it wasn't until 1907, when the French took charge of Indochina, that Angkor Wat became the centerpiece of a restoration project that lasted more than fifty years, until the political climate changed. The natural climate made it a thankless job. During the annual four-month-long rainy season, flooding in the surrounding countryside made the site nearly inaccessible, and the moisture encouraged moss and fungus, vines and trees to grow back in less time than it took to remove them. Although the fighting never touched the ruins, the Vietnam War undid almost all of the restoration accomplished by the French, work that has recently been restarted by Indian archaeologists. During the time the French parted the curtains to reveal a glimpse of the accomplishments of the Khmer civilization, however, they not only uncovered its architectural achievements, but found written records so carefully compiled that it was possible to create an accurate chronology of the people who left them.

Time doesn't seem at all important at Angkor. It is the personality of the people themselves that shines through everywhere in the buildings they created. Their hopes and dreams, their fantasies and nearly every aspect of their everyday life are frozen in time in the soft basalt. Every wall has representations of day-to-day existence, from grand triumphal parades to great conquests, and even circus acrobats and chefs at work with pots, pans, and ladles are depicted. Towers rising like lotus petals have human faces on four sides looking off to every point of the compass.

The Bayon, the sacred shrine of the older town of Angkor Thom, contains fifty-four elaborately carved, massive towers crammed into fifty-six acres (23 ha) and is for all the world like an amusement park funhouse, complete with sculptured heads eight feet (2.4m) high and strange smiling faces at every turn. Some are smiles of welcome from carved dancing girls offering flowers to passersby, but most of the people captured in stone are simply grinning, smirking, or leering, presumably just for the fun of it. Like the Mayans and the Egyptians, the ancient

Khmers didn't seem to think much of bare walls; one of the intricately carved panels at the Bayon even shows in great detail how the walls themselves were built. Slaves supervised by whip-wielding overseers are shown quarrying the stone, sliding the huge blocks across one another to grind them smooth, and carrying them twenty miles (32km) to the building site on poles pushed through holes drilled near the top of each stone.

If the walls of the Khmer temples seem to be bursting with humanity, the buildings of Angkor do not seem to have been built for humans, except possibly to impress them. While it is probable that the original city had wooden houses that have long since disintegrated, only one of the surviving build-ings in the whole complex, a Buddhist monastery, was used for living space. Most of the others didn't even allow space for people to gather. The top floor of the Bayon, for instance, is difficult to reach and so cluttered with its four-sided towers that there is barely room to turn around. The floors below it, as is the case in many of the Khmer buildings, have doors and windows, most of which are fakes, placed there in the interest of symmetry rather than utility. In addition, many of the real doors are so low that, even assuming that the Khmers were unusually short, passing through them would be a good way to get a bump on the head. Most of the spaces, except small galleries and some tiny buildings, had no roofs because the Khmer architects built without mortar

THE FACES (ABOVE AND OPPOSITE PAGE) THAT APPEAR ON ALL FOUR SIDES OF THE BAYON TOWERS WERE ORIGINALLY THOUGHT TO BE IMAGES OF BRAHMA, THE CREATOR OF THE HINDU TRINITY. ACTUALLY, THEY REPRESENT LOKESVARA, A BODHISATTVA, "BUDDHA-TO-BE," WHO AVOIDED THE FINAL CROSSING INTO ENLIGHTENMENT, STAYING BEHIND TO GUIDE MANKIND. ANGKOR THOM, BUILT IN THE LATE TWELFTH CENTURY, IS THE LAST GREAT MONUMENT OF KHMER ARCHITECTURE. IT WAS BUILT BY JAYAVARMAN VII.

and never bothered to stagger the courses of stone to create firm walls. Even though they are made of blocks piled directly on top of one another, however, they are still standing after all these years.

If the Khmers didn't seem to give much thought to making buildings useful, they obviously gave a great deal of thought to making them beautiful. As the principles of building evolved slowly through ancient cultures, the concept of relating a structure to others around it was a long time in coming. Very few of the great buildings of the ancient world show that any thought was given to the open spaces between them and their neighbors as part of the architectural statement. By contrast, Angkor Wat is arguably the world's best example of perfect harmony, both in the relationship of one building to another and to the spaces that separate them.

The city covers an area of more than a square mile (2.6 sq km) and is surrounded by a moat 250 yards (230m) wide. The causeway crossing the water passes through a series of covered galleries toward the temple at the center, which is surrounded by open gardens and reflecting pools. The building is filled with sculptures and reliefs. The third story is on top of a steep pyramid with three almost unclimbable staircases on each side leading up to a gallery whose four corners support huge, highly decorated towers complementing a fifth in the center that soars more than 150 feet (45m) high.

The temple complex at Angkor Wat is a wedding cake of three-headed elephants, seven-headed serpents, lions, cobras, and the garuda, a mythical beast with the body and head of a man but the wings and beak of a bird and sometimes the legs of a lion. The Hindu gods are all there, and so is the great Buddha; humans, both real and imagined, are also represented. One of the longest carved panels in the sanctuary is filled with thousands of gods and demons, which are bigger than life, churning the Sea of Milk with a captive serpent to force the food of immortality, "amrita," to rise to the surface. According to Hindu legend, the object of their quest was finally appropriated by the tortoise who carried the mountains of the world on his back. Some modern interpreters of the myth say that amrita is another word for opium, and suggest that the stone carvers and builders of Angkor found their inspiration in the drug.

OF THE FOUR TOWER GATES, KNOWN AS *GOPARUMS*, AT ANGKOR WAT, THE SO-CALLED ELEPHANT GATE (OPPOSITE PAGE) ON THE WESTERN SIDE IS, AT 257 YARDS (235M), THE WIDEST. THE TOPS OF ITS THREE TOWERS HAVE VANISHED, BUT THE INTERIORS CONTAIN SOME OF THE MOST BEAUTIFUL DECORATIONS IN THE ENTIRE TEMPLE COMPLEX. INTRICATE RELIEFS (LEFT) CARVED ON THE WALLS OF THE OUTER CORRIDORS OF THE BAYON PORTRAY THE GREAT BATTLES OF KHMER HISTORY. OTHER SCENES RECREATED THERE ARE OF EVERYDAY LIFE. THE CREATORS OF THE RELIEFS KNEW NOTHING OF PERSPECTIVE AND INDICATED DISTANCE BY THE POSITIONS OF VARIOUS FIGURES.

THE WEST FACADE OF ANGKOR WAT (OPPOSITE PAGE, TOP), DOMINATED BY THE ELEPHANT GATE, INCLUDES A LONG CORRIDOR THAT IS RAISED ON A PLATFORM SOME THIRTEEN FEET (4M) HIGH AND FILLED WITH RELIGIOUS IMAGES. INSIDE, BEYOND THE GATE, A PERFECTLY STRAIGHT SACRED ROAD RUNS FOR 519 YARDS (475M) TOWARD A GREAT TEMPLE. RELIEFS (OPPOSITE PAGE, BOTTOM) IN THE TEMPLE AT ANGKOR WAT, ORIGINALLY GILDED WITH GOLD LEAF, ARE BASED ON RELIGIOUS THEMES FOR THE INSTRUCTION OF THE PEOPLE. THE GODDESSES, CALLED *DEVATAS*, ARE SHOWN WITH THEIR FACES, HANDS, AND BODIES IN FRONTAL POSITION, BUT THEIR FEET ALWAYS POINT SIDEWAYS. THE *APSARA* (LEFT), THE CELESTIAL DANCER OF ANGKOR WAT, IS A SYMBOL OF KHMER CULTURE. AN EARLY FRENCH EXPLORER, WHO ESTIMATED THAT THERE WERE 1,750 OF THEM IN THE TEMPLE, SAID, "TO ME THEY ARE GRACE PERSONIFIED, THE HIGHEST EXPRESSION OF FEMININITY EVER CONCEIVED BY THE HUMAN MIND." BUILT ON A HILL NEAR THE BANKS OF THE SIEM REAP RIVER, THE TOWERS OF ANGKOR WAT (ABOVE) SOAR ABOVE THE CAMBODIAN PLAIN. ANGKOR WAT IS THE LARGEST RELIGIOUS MONUMENT IN THE WORLD AND HENRI MOUHOT, WHO REDISCOVERED IT IN 1860, WROTE THAT "IT IS GRANDER THAN ANYTHING LEFT TO US BY GREECE OR ROME."

EASTER ISLAND

The images at Angkor are easily interpreted because there are so many representations of Hinduism and Buddhism all over Asia. At about the same time Angkor Wat was being built, an enigmatic civilization was well into its decline on an island in the Pacific more than nine thousand miles (14,400km) away, and the monuments it left behind are as mysterious as anything else on earth. Almost from the fateful Easter Sunday in 1722 when this tiny spit of land 1,750 miles (2,800km) west of the South American coast was discovered by Dutch explorers, Easter Island and its lost civilization have confounded every attempt to discover their origins.

If no one knows who the inhabitants of Easter Island were, no one disagrees that they probably developed one of the most sophisticated Neolithic cultures on earth. Their descendants described their forty-five-square-mile (117 sq km) island as the Navel of the World, and as far as they knew, it was the only dry land there was. If they sailed south, the nearest land was 3,250 miles (5,200km) away; to the north, the trip to the nearest land was 3,000 miles (4,800km) and to the east it was 1,750 miles (2,800km). Their nearest neighbors to the west were 750 miles (1,200km) away on a tiny speck of land called Ducie Island that even modern mariners using satellite navigation have trouble finding. Yet out there in the middle of the ocean, prehistoric people created a written language, carved hundreds of monolithic statues, and built temples whose sites hint at an uncommon knowledge of astronomy.

By the time Europeans discovered Easter Island, the ancient people had already disappeared and the people left behind had lost the skills of their predecessors. Over a century and a half, most of the islanders were carried off as slaves; by the 1870s, there were only about a hundred of them left. Christian missionaries began encouraging them to forget about such heathen ideas as graven images, and by the time anthropologists began studying the Easter Islanders, there was no oral history of their past, except for half-forgotten myths. There are, however, clues to their ancestral background. The island's discoverers were told that it was originally settled by a king named Hoto Matua who was the first of fifty-seven generations of monarchs. The story goes on to say that the original people fell into two groups known as the Short Ears and the Long Ears, who were usually at war with one another. That began a debate that is still going on: the Long Ears, said one theory, were obviously Polynesians, well known for their practice of stretching their earlobes; the Short Ears, the theory continued, must have come from Peru. If that suggests that the Easter Island civilization was a combination of Pacific islanders and remnants of the South American civilizations, however, there was no way to prove it.

The best known modern theory comes from the Norwegian archaeologist Thor Heyerdahl, who claimed that the Polynesians themselves originally came from South America and settled on Easter Island in the sixth century. This idea was part of a larger thesis that the natives of North and South America had learned everything they knew from early Vikings and that the Pacific cultures were simply an extension of the process. To prove it, Heyerdahl sailed halfway across the Pacific, far beyond Easter Island, on a balsa log raft called *Kon-Tiki* that he built from plans of similar vessels used by the Tiahuanaco people of ancient Peru. He believed that Easter Island had been originally settled by the Tiahuanacos and that the first Hawaiians were an Indian tribe from the American Pacific Northwest. His dramatic sea voyage only proved they could have sailed that far, not that they did; in the case of Easter Island, he also cited evidence that the language spoken there was similar to some in South America, as was the written language, which, like so many others, is still unreadable. Whether all Polynesians originated in the West or if Easter Island was a meeting place for wanderers from both Asia and the Americas is still the subject of heated debate.

The search for the Long Ears and the Short Ears involves much more than simply trying to figure out where they came from. Even though Easter Island is one of the most remote spots on earth, it has seen more archaeological research than any other site in

ABOUT A THOUSAND OF THE
HUGE SCULPTURES CALLED *MOAI*
WERE CARVED BY THE EASTER
ISLANDERS, WHO WERE AT TIMES
IN THE VIOLENT HISTORY OF
THEIR CULTURE OUTNUMBERED
BY THE MONUMENTS. WHILE THE
STATUES ALL RESEMBLE EACH
OTHER ON THE WHOLE, THERE
ARE SUBTLE DIFFERENCES FROM
ONE TO THE NEXT.

THE DEEP-SET EYES OF THE *MOAI* (RIGHT) GIVE THEM A THOUGHTFUL, MYSTERIOUS LOOK, AND THE VARIATIONS OF SHADOWS AS THE SUN MOVES ACROSS THE SKY GIVE THEM A KIND OF LIFE. THE MOUTH IS ALWAYS REPRESENTED WITH PURSED LIPS, WHICH MAKES THE FIGURE APPEAR TO BE SITTING IN GRIM JUDGMENT. THE STATUES (BELOW) OF THE EASTER ISLANDERS WEIGH UP TO SEVERAL TONS, BUT WERE NONETHELESS MOVED GREAT DISTANCES AND RAISED ONTO ALTARS, CALLED *AHUS*, THAT WERE AS MUCH AS FIFTEEN FEET (4.6M) HIGH. MANY WERE ALSO GIVEN HUGE STONE TOPKNOTS, ALWAYS RED, ALTHOUGH THE MOAI THEMSELVES ARE YELLOWISH GRAY.

the Pacific area—more, in fact, than the alleged sites of most other lost civilizations in other parts of the world. The work has been going on since 1866, and after the 1960s several of the sites and ceremonial centers were restored. But most of the strange stone statues, called "moai," are still where they were found, buried up to their necks in dirt and rubble and staring out to sea. They were all originally standing on the tops of stone platforms, but the legends say that in the battles between the island's two tribes, enemies provoked one another by toppling each other's moai. It must have kept them quite busy because there are hundreds of them; the few that are standing upright today were returned to their perches only in recent times.

All of these strange statues are carved from volcanic rock; the Rano Raraku volcano in the southeast seems to be the major source of the stone. How they were moved down the mountainside to their resting places miles away is still not adequately explained, but it is obvious that all of the stones were shaped at the quarries. The mountain is still littered with moai, including one almost seventy feet (21m) high, many of which are unfinished, still attached to the rock of the mountainside as though waiting for the carver to come back. Although the moai have subtle differences, most of them look alike: a human figure with a three-foot (0.9m) base. Arms dangle stiffly at their sides and the hands spread across a protruding stomach. Their outsize rectangular heads all have heavy brows and big noses, the lips are thin, and the chin is as prominent as the brow. Breasts and navels are indicated and many moai have designs, thought to represent tattoos, on their backs.

By the time the Europeans arrived, all building had stopped and the people who carved the moai had vanished. While the people's origin is mysterious, the eighteenth-century Easter Islanders nevertheless had a legend that explained what had become of them. According to the tale, one of the Long Ears' construction projects involved digging a wide trench across the island to protect themselves against surprise attacks by their short-eared enemies. It was filled with brush and logs that they

© Wolfgang Kaehler

MORE THAN SEVENTY UNFINISHED STATUES STAND GUARD OVER THE VOLCANO CRATER OF RANO RARAKU, WHERE NEARLY ALL OF THE EASTER ISLAND *MOAI* WERE MADE. MOST OF THE STANDING STATUES ELSEWHERE ON THE ISLAND WERE TOPPLED BY LATER GENERATIONS, BUT NONE OF THE RANO RARAKU GIANTS HAVE BEEN DISTURBED.

planned to set on fire if they were threatened. When the Short Ears finally decided to attack, they sent a company of soldiers across the ditch to stay hidden until their main army gathered on the other side and started goading the Long Ears into lighting their fire, which they did. After the fire was lit, the concealed Short Ears emerged and forced the Long Ears into the trench, burning all but three to death. Like most legends, this was almost too fantastic to believe, but in 1956, an international team of archaeologists organized by Thor Heyerdahl found an artificial ditch filled with ashes and charcoal suggesting a very hot fire had once burned there. Carbon dating told them that the trench itself was dug in about A.D. 400, which pushed back the original estimates of the earliest settlement. It was also determined that the fire occurred some 350 years ago, not long before the European explorers began arriving.

ANAKENA BEACH WAS THE PRIVATE PRESERVE OF THE HOTU MATUA, THE LEGENDARY FIRST KING OF EASTER ISLAND. IT WAS SET ASIDE FOR HIS EXCLUSIVE USE AND EXCEPT FOR HIS WIVES AND CHILDREN AND THEIR SERVANTS, ANYONE FOUND THERE WAS KILLED ON THE SPOT.

Chapter 7

Magic Circles

Stonehenge and Ancient Britain

The British Isles are lands of myth and legend, historically populated by witches, sorcerers, and fantastic creatures conjured up over the centuries by various people attempting to explain the origins of the ancient Britons. The reality is proving to be as fascinating as any of the tales of magic, and the clues to a lost civilization of early Britons are beginning to fit together in remarkable ways.

ANCIENT BRITAIN

In the sixteenth century, when England's Queen Elizabeth I began exporting British civilization and culture to the rest of the world, her subjects were just beginning to look seriously into the past for clues of an earlier civilization in their own country. Up until then, nearly everyone believed that the country's most visible monument, a circle of 162 massive stone blocks on the Salisbury Plain called Stonehenge, had been transported there from Ireland by the great magician Merlin. The story said that the Britons invaded the neighboring island and, after defeating the Irish, went on a sight-seeing tour that took them to the top of a mountain where giants had erected a huge stone temple. It seemed a perfect trophy, but it was far too big for any of them to move until Merlin cast a magic spell that gave them the strength to do the job. The temple was thus dismantled and reconstructed back home in England. Naturally, not everyone believed the tale. One Italian historian was appalled that the British should extol their own ancestors "above the nobleness of the Romans and Macedonians, enhancing them with most impudent lying." The English were unruffled; an Elizabethan historian, with a perfectly straight face, put the story in perspective when he wrote, "Almost everything that is related about bringing these stones from Ireland is fictional. For everybody, however ignorant, ought to know that these enormous stones—which our own age, so short of talent, is unable to shift—were brought by Merlin from some quarry nearby with remarkable ingenuity and using clever inventions. . . . It would have been beyond the ability of the Romans to move things of such weight from Ireland."

The building that apparently once stood there is on level ground in the center of a great enclosure surrounded by a 330-foot (100m) ditch. A causeway that is about seventy-five feet (23m) wide comes out of the plain from the northeast, passing several huge

place where ancient kings were crowned. Credit for the work was given to Danish Vikings, to Anglo-Saxons with skills brought from northern Germany, and, of course, to the usual wandering Phoenicians. A more recent thesis is that the silent stones were once a huge observatory for ancient astronomers incorporating the learning of Egyptians and Greeks. The idea that the stones were a prehistoric digital computer even led one scientist to claim that they were moved around the ring to make mathematical calculations and that the practice gave the world the game of checkers. For all the words and all the speculation, Stonehenge is still as mysterious as ever, and for all anyone knows, Merlin just might have had a hand in it.

It is apparent that it was once a single building and although more than half the stones are missing and others are broken and have fallen over, it is still easy to see the form it took. The complex is surrounded by some thirty squared upright stones forming a perfect circle about one hundred feet (30m) in diameter. The monoliths are seven feet (2.1m) wide and support horizontal stone lintels whose flat tops are sixteen feet (4.8m) above the ground. No mortar was used, but the stones are held together with small projections in the upright portions that fit snugly into holes carved into the bases of the lintels. The horizontal stones are connected to one another by projections that are slid into slots in the same way that wooden flooring is held in place (tongue and groove). Inside is another group of smaller upright blocks—of a completely different kind of stone—without lintels, forming a circle seventy-five feet (23m) in diameter around five upright groupings resembling the outer ring. The inner group forms a horseshoe open to the northeast and it, in turn, encloses another similar horseshoe of shorter square stones. In the center of it all are the remains of what seems to have been a sixteen-foot (4.8m) altar stone.

The building that apparently once stood there is on level ground in the center of a great enclosure surrounded by a 330-foot (100m) ditch. A causeway that is about seventy-five feet (23m) wide comes out of the plain from the northeast passing several huge

© Everett C. Johnson/Leo de Wys

LEFT AND BELOW: THE OUTER CIRCLE OF STONEHENGE IS MADE OF A KIND OF SANDSTONE CALLED *SARSEN*. ITS THIRTY SQUARED UPRIGHTS SUPPORTED HORIZONTAL LINTELS IN A PERFECT CIRCLE ONE HUNDRED FEET (31M) IN DIAMETER. INSIDE WAS A SEVENTY-FIVE-FOOT (23M) CIRCLE OF SMALLER UPRIGHT BLUESTONES OF WHICH ONLY SIX OF THE ORIGINAL SIXTY ARE STILL STANDING. OVER THE CENTURIES STONEHENGE HAS BEEN ACCEPTED AS A KIND OF RELIGIOUS SHRINE. IN RECENT YEARS, THOUGH, IT HAS BECOME FASHIONABLE TO REGARD IT AS A LABORATORY FOR ANCIENT ASTRONOMERS. THERE IS NO SOLID EVIDENCE TO SUPPORT EITHER THEORY.

© Michael J. Howell/Envision

© Cindy A. Pavlinac

stone slabs and three rings of fifty-six regularly spaced pits, which have been variously described as burial sites and a means of counting years (to predict lunar eclipses) or months (to anticipate the setting of the summer new moon). The pits are called "Aubrey holes" in honor of John Aubrey, a slightly eccentric seventeenth-century renaissance man who was fascinated by the idea that Stonehenge and other similar sites were built by a lost civilization of Britons and not by any outsiders.

This theory was an obsession he picked up as a teenager when he first saw the great monoliths near the village of Avebury, about twenty miles (6.1km) north of Stonehenge, and noted that it was "very strange that such an eminent antiquity should lie so long unregarded." Stonehenge was already quite well known, but in Aubrey's opinion, "Avebury did as much excell Stonehenge as a cathedral does a parish church." When King Charles II heard Aubrey's opinion, he ordered a written report, which was expanded into a book called *Monumenta Brittannica*. In spite of the book's Latin title, it set out to prove that the more than nine hundred stone circles found from the tip of Wales to the top of Scotland and even across the Irish Sea existed well outside the limits of Roman Britain and often ap-

pear in places where no alien cultures penetrated until long after the monuments had been reduced to mysterious piles of stone.

It was quite obvious to Aubrey that the stone rings were the remains of temples and it was just as obvious that they were temples built by druids, the priestly class of ancient Britain. It hit the right spot of patriotic pride for Charles and his subjects, and in the three centuries since Aubrey died, his book is still unfinished and no one has come up with a better theory. He may have arrived at the right answer by asking the wrong questions, or at least the sort of questions not generally associated with scientific research. Early in his research, he reduced the problem to mathematics, comparing one ruin to another and combining them, as he put it, into "a kind of equation." Later, as time began running out, he put his faith in a stone tablet with writing no one could read. Some scholars felt that the letters were a form of Greek, but Aubrey was sure they had been chiseled by druids and, in the absence of a translation, his opinion was as good as anyone's. The clincher, as far as he was concerned, were the sparrows nesting in holes in the Stonehenge stones. The druids, he said, routinely had conversations with birds and he was certain that they had cut holes to encourage birds to nest there and bring them news of the outside world. During all his research, scientific and otherwise, Aubrey never wavered from his original idea that the main cathedral of the druids was not Stonehenge but Avebury. He may have been right about that, too. Avebury was larger by far than any of the other ancient sites in the British Isles, but most of it has been obscured by a village that has been built in the center of it as well as by a highway and farms.

When the Saxons arrived in the thirteenth century, the Britons found Avebury a handy ready-made fortress, and there is evidence that the invaders took it as their own because their main military road cut through the heart of the ancient temple complex. It wasn't until a century later, when zealous Christians began burying the stones to get the hated symbols of paganism out of sight, that the real damage to the site started; in later centuries more practical people repossessed them to build barns and houses. Even John Aubrey's enthusiastic descriptions of Avebury's importance didn't stop the destruction, and it wasn't until the 1860s that serious excavation and restoration began. It has since been estimated that the ditch that surrounded it was dug in about 2000 B.C. and that 200,000 tons of chalk were removed to create it. The estimate of the work involved is staggering: researchers studying the ditch have concluded that it was dug using antlers, bits of bone, and bare hands by people who had no knowledge of metal tools of any sort. The stone slabs weighed as much as forty tons (36t), and it may have taken the strength of two hundred people to raise each of them upright. How they were transported there is anybody's guess.

There are still people who feel it must all have been the result of magic spells. Aubrey was convinced that the druids had conversations with birds, but that was only one of the strange things of which they were said to be capable. The Rollright Stones in Oxfordshire are quite possibly the most enduring testament to their power, at least if the story about them is to be believed. Rollright is a perfect circle of about seventy stones with another strangely twisted monolith, called the King Stone, overlooking them. According to the story, which is still widely believed, the lone monolith is an ancient king turned to stone by a druid witch and the circle is formed by his soldiers, similarly cursed. Other monoliths nearby are traitorous knights who led their king into the hands of the witch, and it is said they can still be heard whispering to each other about how they themselves were betrayed. As recently as the beginning of the twentieth century, local people swore that the soldier stones moved down the hill to drink at the spring at midnight on New Year's day. For centuries there have been regular reports of moonlight witch's sabbaths around the King Stone. Of course, such things don't happen in the 1990s. Or do they? Just to be on the safe side, it might be best to avoid the stone circles of Britain on the night of April 30, Walpurgis Night, when the secrets of the ancients might be revealed in ways best left shrouded in mystery.

YOU COULD MAKE IT UP

Digging for the past is a relatively new science; in the middle ages no one bothered with such explorations. If picking up a shovel seemed like ungentlemanly labor, however, picking up a pen and speculating about ancient history was not. In twelfth-century England, Geoffrey of Monmouth gave his country a new set of roots when he fantasized that civilization had arrived in Britain from ancient Troy. His books, which were the first to tell the stories of King Arthur and King Lear, were accepted as fact for generations. They also included the tale of a Trojan prince named Brutus whom Geoffrey claimed had landed on the south coast of Devon in 1170 B.C.—Geoffrey was quite specific about the date—and established a colony similar to one in Asia Minor. The theory made perfect sense when the author pointed out that

Brutus had named the land Britain in honor of himself. Some years later, the University of Cambridge commissioned another history, for which the dons invented a Mediterranean king they named Cantaber. According to their account, Cantaber trekked across Spain and eventually wound up in England, where he decided to settle down in a place that was named Cambridge in his honor. (For the record, the name Britain was coined by Julius Caesar, who saw the similarity between the islanders and their cousins across the Channel in Britanny; and Cambridge, although the site of one of the earliest settlements in the British Isles, also owes it name to the Romans. The university, which its first history says was founded by King Cantaber, was actually established in the 1280s by Christian missionaries.)

© Cindy A. Pavinac

Lost and Found

The Search for the Past

Before 1859, when Charles Darwin changed the way mankind thought about its origins with the publication of his *Origin of Species*, not much serious thought was given to searching for hidden clues to past civilizations except for the ones mentioned in the Bible. And even though searchers have been combing through the desert sands of the Near East longer than almost anywhere else, there are still ancient cities waiting to be found.

The Islamic holy book, the Koran, speaks of a place called Iram, which it says was "a many-columned city...whose like has not been built in the entire land." The Alexandrian geographer Claudius Ptolemy wrote in the second century A.D. of a similar place called Ubar. A sixth-century Arabic historian, Al-Hamandi, offers yet another description of a city that was an "imitation of paradise," with impressive buildings, huge groves of fruit trees, and more wealth than any other city that existed in ancient times. There is little question that Iram and Ubar are one and the same; the Koran relates that its inhabitants were condemned for their sinful ways and that Allah consequently destroyed them and their city.

The source of the city's wealth was frankincense, and the trees that produce the resin still grow in the Quara Mountains of southern Oman. The presence of these trees was a strong clue that the destroyed city must be buried somewhere nearby. It was also the only clue. T. E. Lawrence, known as Lawrence of Arabia, was intrigued by it and was organizing a search for Ubar when he died. A few years later, another British explorer, Bertram Thomas, guided by bedouins along what they said was the road to Ubar, found the ruins of an old fort, but no city.

In 1981, Nicholas Clapp, a Los Angeles film-maker fascinated by the mystery, put Thomas' account together with Ptolemy's map and concluded that the city was still under the sands of Arabia and that the only way to find it was with space technology. Using enhanced computer images from the U.S. Landsat spacecraft and the French SPOT satellite, scientists at the Jet Propulsion Laboratory in California plotted tracks of ancient caravan routes that seemed to converge on a huge sand dune near the water hole to which the bedouins had led Bertram Thomas. In 1990, researchers on the ground found evidence of frankincense trade over many of the routes and eventually, using more satellite tracking, narrowed their search to a single spot that near the end of 1991 yielded the remains of a

city that predates any other in southern Arabia. Preliminary dating of the ruins and its artifacts suggest they are at least four thousand years old, and the buildings themselves seem to fit the Koran's description of the lost city of Iram.

The dig has also shown why ancient writings, including the *Arabian Nights*, say Iram was destroyed in a sudden cataclysm. It was originally built on top of a huge limestone cavern that collapsed, suddenly plunging the buildings into a huge hole that was quickly filled in by the desert sands. Without an eye in the sky, it may have been lost there forever.

The same satellite-borne radar is at work tracking the fabled silk road in northwestern China, and airborne instruments have found buried buildings in the Chaco Canyon of New Mexico that predate the first known Anasazi cliff dwellings, possibly by thousands of years. Surveys from the air have found thousand-year-old footpaths under volcanic ash in the mountains of Costa Rica and ancient Mayan roads in the Yucatán and Guatemala. The special cameras carried by the space shuttles and mounted on satellites go far beyond what the naked eye can see from the ground or from anywhere else. Using thermal wavelengths, they can detect spots where plant growth was affected by ancient farmers and find places where the soil has been compacted by wandering people. Almost none of this technology is much older than two decades. When the first Landsat Satellite was launched in 1972 to create more accurate maps of the earth's surface, it couldn't pick out an object less than two hundred feet (61m) wide. Although later versions are twice as accurate—the French SPOT satellite can see objects below that are fifty feet (15m) wide—there is a growing need for even more sophisticated cameras and radar. In the 1980s NASA went so far as to add an archaeologist to its staff.

It was NASA that found the ancient roads in Chaco Canyon when its resident archaeologist, Dr. Thomas Sever, mounted infrared cameras to an airplane and flew over it. He had a road map to follow in the form of a series of photographs taken by no less a person than Charles Lindbergh back in

DEEP FREEZE

The remains of many of the ancient civilizations that have given up their secrets have been preserved over the centuries in hot, dry climates. But not all of them. After peeling away layers of strange mounds at Pazyryk, a river valley in western Siberia, Russian archaeologists found the entrance to the tomb of a king who had ruled the nomadic tribes of the far north in the fifth century B.C. It was crammed with the skeletons of horses and the remains of heavy wooden carts, tents, and bronze pots. Beyond was the huge tomb itself, with elaborate rugs, embroidery, and wall hangings as bright and colorful as they had been when the chamber was sealed twenty-five centuries ago. The bodies of the king and his female companion, in coffins of hollowed logs, were also in a remarkable state of preservation because the tomb was filled with a solid block of ice. The scientists removed them from cold storage after pouring boiling water on the ice and pumping out the remaining moisture.

THE OLD CITY OF JERUSALEM, SILENT FOR CENTURIES, BEGAN TO INTEREST FRENCH ARCHAEOLOGISTS IN 1850; IN THE 1860S ENGLAND'S QUEEN VICTORIA SENT A TEAM OF SCIENTISTS TO FIND OUT MORE. REALLY SERIOUS RESEARCH INTO JERUSALEM'S PAST, HOWEVER, DID NOT BEGIN UNTIL THE CREATION OF THE STATE OF ISRAEL IN 1948.

1929 that showed lines that might have been roads; the more sensitive cameras that Sever carried proved it. New sensors are also capable of finding old irrigation ditches that have been silted over for thousands of years as well as ancient riverbeds that have disappeared. In 1981, radar equipment aboard the space shuttle *Columbia* found prehistoric rivers five feet (1.5m) under the sands of the Sahara Desert and subsequent excavations found evidence that humans were living there more than 200,000 years ago.

It is quite possible, of course, that 200,000 years from now archaeologists using who knows what kind of sophisticated technology will be looking for clues to our civilizations. It is likely that rather than studying the rise and fall of twentieth-century cultures, they'll be tracing the history of technology itself. The trend has already begun, but it is a concept that didn't begin until the 1930s, when treasure hunters were replaced by scientists in the search for lost civilizations. The prime mover in the field was Gordon Childe, a British archaeologist who theorized that human history wasn't so much a matter of clashing armies and palace intrigues as it was the development of technologies that gave the armies better weapons and the nobles a reliable food supply. Historians, he said, should be concerned with the evolution of animal herding and farming, pottery making, and hunting because these are the things that made civilization possible. He called it the "Neolithic Revolution," a stage in the development of mankind when people began using their brains to produce food surpluses and free other brains to create cities and civilizations. Childe's pronouncements have been debated ever since he first made them, but almost every search for lost civilizations in the last half century has been based on them, even if to disprove them.

An integral component in proving or disproving anything about the ancient world lies in determining the ages of the objects and information that are discovered. When the search for lost civilizations began, written records and inscriptions in Egyptian temples and burial sites were used to date civilizations that existed as far back as 3000 B.C. Clay tablets were related to Egyptian writings and Sumerian records eventually allowed reasonably accurate dating to extend another thousand years into antiquity.

Other parts of the ancient world—China, the Americas, the Indus Valley, and Africa—had no contact with the Egyptians, and connections could not be made between their records and known chronologies that would date the cultures. Of course, this comparative method has no relevance within the long period of time that was conveniently labeled "prehistory." Other methods were employed in the effort to affix a year to certain discoveries. Some nineteenth-century Americans experimented with counting rings of fossilized trees, and in Scandinavia at the same time they were analyzing debris left behind by melting glaciers as well as pollen buried for centuries in peat bogs.

It wasn't until 1949 that an accurate scientific method was established to date findings. Dr. Willard F. Libby of the University of Chicago announced that with the completion of research that

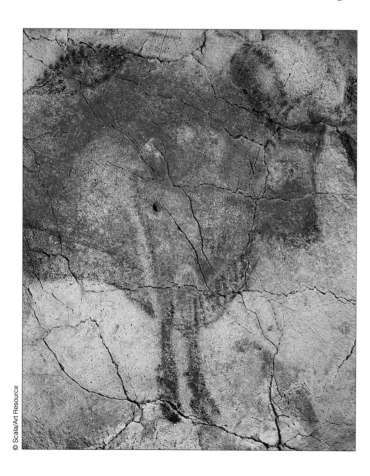

THE STONE AGE ART IN THE CAVERNS AT ALTAMIRA, SPAIN, HAS BEEN PRESERVED FOR THOUSANDS OF YEARS BY CONSTANT TEMPERATURE AND UNCHANGING HUMIDITY. THE PALEOLITHIC ARTIST WHO PAINTED THIS BISON TOOK ADVANTAGE OF THE CONTOURS OF THE CAVE ITSELF TO ADD DEPTH AND CREATE A THREE-DIMENSIONAL LOOK.

had begun thirty years earlier, he had perfected the "clock that runs backwards"—radiocarbon dating. This analysis was made possible by Marie Curie's discovery of radium in 1898 and the observation that radioactive elements decay at a predictable rate.

Libby hypothesized that the amount of the radioactive isotope carbon-14 (radiocarbon) present on the earth is constant because the cosmic radiation that changes nitrogen atoms to radiocarbon has been constant for hundreds of thousands of years, long enough for this exchange to reach a steady state. This led him to think that there is as much radiocarbon in any living matter today as there would have been in similar organisms thousands of years ago. However, when a plant or animal dies it stops absorbing radiocarbon atoms, and the radiocarbon already present continues to decay. Because radiocarbon and ordinary carbon atoms are absorbed by living things in identical ways, the ratio of these types of carbon is the same in every organism. Analysis of organic remains can determine how much ordinary carbon is present, therefore determining how much radiocarbon there was when the plant or animal died, and how much radiocarbon is left. This information, when compiled with the known rate of disintegration (half-life) of radiocarbon, can be used to determine when the organism died.

But having solved one of their most perplexing problems, modern archaeologists are faced with quite another that might not be as easily solved. The past, they are discovering, is much simpler to deal with than the present. When the Vietnam War shut down their work on the Cambodian temples at Angkor, the war itself didn't destroy any of them, but for twenty years hundreds of sculptures and fragments were stolen. The war in Lebanon also encouraged thieves who even used bulldozers to get at Phoenician gold and Byzantine mosaics, and the bombardment of Iraq hit at the very cradle of civilization.

If war is hell, even peaceful sites that attract well-meaning visitors by the busload are in big trouble. The prehistoric caves of Lascaux in France have been closed to the public and visitors are shown

© Wim Swaan/FPG International

THE STATUE OF TUTANKHAMEN AT THE TEMPLE OF KARNAK HAS BEEN SLIGHTLY DAMAGED OVER THE YEARS, BUT HIS TOMB WAS UNTOUCHED AND REMAINED INTACT FOR THOUSANDS OF YEARS. MANY OF THE TOMBS OF HIS ANCESTORS WERE LOOTED AND DESTROYED LONG BEFORE HE WAS BORN.

replicas of them instead, and not long ago a volunteer removing grafitti from a French cave also washed away a painting thousands of years old. And the vandalism goes beyond such willful acts as graffiti painting and littering. The tomb of King Tutankhamen in Egypt is losing the original luster of its painted walls because of the breath and the sweat of thousands of people who pass through it and leave behind a layer of moisture and salt on the surface. The same problem almost completely destroyed the paintings in the tomb of Queen Nefertiti before it was closed to prevent more damage. Worried that the living will destroy ancient monuments to the dead, many archaeologists are suggesting that once a ruin is excavated, photographed, and cataloged it should be hidden away again. In other words, there is a growing theory that lost civilizations are safer when they remain outside of the (often destructive) reach of modern inquiry.

Lost Civilizations at a Glance

Illinois River
Ohio River

Chaco Canyon

Mississippi River

Teotihuácan

Palenque

Chichén Itzá

Amazon River

Machu Picchu
Cuzco

Easter Island

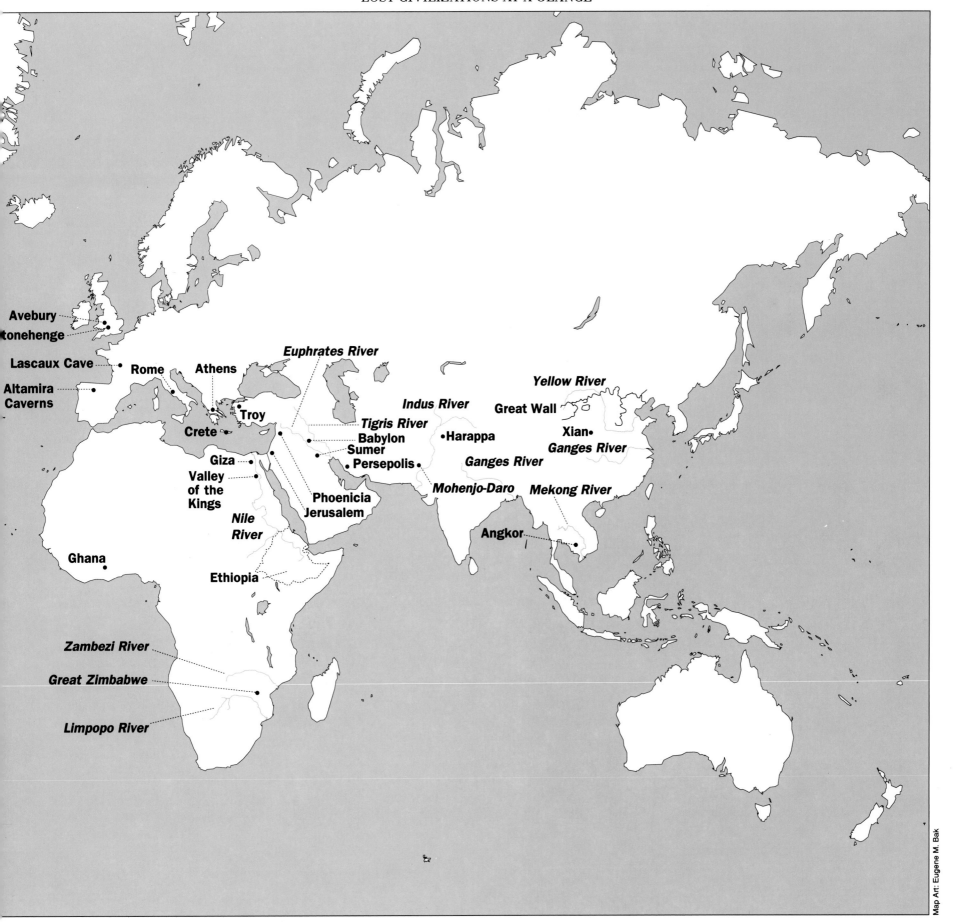

Avebury
Stonehenge

Lascaux Cave

Altamira
Caverns

Rome   Athens

Euphrates River

Yellow River

Indus River   Great Wall

Troy

Tigris River
Babylon   Xian
Crete   Sumer   *Ganges River*
•Harappa

Giza   •Persepolis
Valley   *Ganges River*
of the   Phoenicia
Kings   Jerusalem   *Mohenjo-Daro*   *Mekong River*

Nile
River

Ghana

Ethiopia   Angkor

Zambezi River

Great Zimbabwe

Limpopo River

Map Art: Eugene M. Bak

Index